W9-CEE-010

# RUN FAST.
## COOK FAST
# EAT SLOW.

# RUN FAST. COOK FAST EAT SLOW.

## QUICK-FIX RECIPES FOR HANGRY ATHLETES

### SHALANE FLANAGAN & ELYSE KOPECKY

PHOTOGRAPHY BY ALAN WEINER

RODALE.

Copyright © 2018 by Shalane Flanagan and Elyse Kopecky

All rights reserved.
Published in the United States by Rodale, an imprint of the Crown Publishing Group,
a division of Penguin Random House LLC, New York.
crownpublishing.com
rodalebooks.com

Rodale and the Rodale colophon are trademarks of Penguin Random House LLC.

Library of Congress Cataloging-in-Publication Data is available.

ISBN 978-1-63565-191-1
Ebook ISBN 978-1-63565-192-8

Printed in China

Cover and interior design by Rae Ann Spitzenberger
Photographs by Alan Weiner
Additional image credits: page 12: Jordan Beckett; page 42: Porter Binks for NYRR;
pages 58 and 192: Jon Wellings; page 145: PhotoRun for NYRR;
page 238: Adam Hunger for NYRR; page 240: Liz Goodman;
page 241: Michelle Adams; page 242: Stefania Curto.
Cover photographs by Alan Weiner (top) and Peter Yang (bottom)

10 9 8

First Edition

*To the running community, for your faith,*
*loving support, and encouragement.*
*—Shalane*

*For Lily and Rylan, my sweet little*
*sidekicks in the kitchen.*
*Feeding you nourishing meals*
*every day brings me endless joy.*
*—Elyse*

# CONTENTS

*Running has the power to heal.*
*Running unites.*
*Running creates community.*
*Running nourishes the soul.*
*Run for lifelong friendships.*
*Run for health.*
*Run for happiness.*
*Running clears the mind.*
*Running strengthens the body.*
*Running is hard work.*
*Hard work is rewarding.*
*Running should be enjoyed.*

*Relish every step.*

*xoxo,*

Shalane

*Food has the power to heal.*
*Food unites.*
*Good food brings people together.*
*Food is the heartbeat of communities.*
*Real food nourishes our bodies and minds.*
*Food is health.*
*Health is happiness.*
*Cooking for others is the greatest gift.*
*Cooking is meditative and restorative.*
*Cooking is hard work.*
*Hard work tastes amazing.*
*Food should be enjoyed.*

*Relish every bite.*

*xoxo,*

Elyse

# INTRODUCTION

**W**hen we began writing our first book, *Run Fast. Eat Slow.* in 2014, we knew we had an important message that could help runners. But it wasn't until we set out on our book tour 2 years later that we fully understood what our first cookbook meant to the running community.

From San Francisco to Seattle, Portland to Chicago, and Charlotte to New York City, we ran with you, shared bites from the book, and heard which recipes had become a staple in your homes. Crowds cheered when we explained why healthy food isn't just kale juice, but also a juicy burger. And we heard testimonials like this:

> *It was a dream come true to run with you last week!! Y'all are promoting such a critical message for athletes, especially female runners. As a member of UNC's cross-country team, and a Girls on the Run coach, I have seen far too many women and girls struggle to establish healthy eating habits to match their training. In fact, I think it is more difficult to find a female runner at the high school or college level who doesn't suffer from athletic amenorrhea than one who does. I hope that you all are able to reach as many athletes as possible with your cookbook and book tour!*
>
> **–EMMA MARIE ASTRIKE-DAVIS,** *UNC CHAPEL HILL STUDENT*

It was so satisfying to learn that high school and college runners, working moms, and even elite athletes who'd gotten caught in harmful diet trends or disordered eating habits were reading our book cover to cover and discovering the benefits of indulging in real food (read more of your letters starting on page 240).

One of the last stops on our tour—Chapel Hill—was the one that turned on the lightbulb for the book in your hands.

It was a nostalgic stop for us. UNC Chapel Hill is where we met more than 18 years ago—freshman year on the cross-country team—and what could be better than snacking on Super-hero Muffins (page 60) as we drove east from Charlotte to our destination. We waved at our old college house on Green Street (still standing!) and noticed the frat boys on Franklin Street looked exactly the same (some styles never change!).

We made our way to the Fleet Feet Carrboro store to lead a run before our talk. Runners were standing in packs by the front door, many decked out in *Run Fast. Eat Slow.* tank tops. The Fleet Feet staff used a megaphone to welcome everyone, and we attempted to squeeze the crowd into a selfie photo. Soon we were off! The run across our college campus was filled with chatter—your infectious enthusiasm had our hearts thumping—and as soon as it was over, we found pen and paper and started jotting down ideas for this book. Suddenly, in Chapel Hill, all the fan mail, stories shared on the runs, and audience Q&As were culminating in a not-so-subtle message: "Shalane, Elyse—write another cookbook! And this time, make it for the high-speed lives runners lead on *and* off the track." It was like a starter gun: We realized there was more work to be done, more athletes to reach, more recipes to write, and more Can't Beet Me Smoothies (page 52) to share!

Tossing out ingrained food phobias and a dependency on processed foods isn't easy, but this book proves that quick and nourishing aren't mutually exclusive. You live a life on-the-go, and nutritious food can go with you. That food need not be time-consuming, bland, or boring. We've designed each recipe in this book to be fast and approachable without compromising flavor or nutrition.

If you're a young athlete, busy student, working parent, beginner cook, or competitive runner, *Run Fast. Cook Fast. Eat Slow.* will help you get nourishing meals on the table every day.

Thank you for sharing your stories of dedication and perseverance. You inspired everything in these pages.

GET READY TO FUEL YOUR BEST LIFE.

*Shalane and Elyse leading a run in Portland, Oregon, at a* Run Fast. Eat Slow. *book tour event hosted by Nike Running.*

## SHALANE'S REAL FOOD STORY

When I moved off the track, from racing 5,000 m and 10,000 m distances to the marathon, my training required doubling the amount of miles I was accustomed to. This was the first time I actually realized that my diet and the food I was putting in my body were crucial to getting me through this additional training. Running 17 miles a day or a grueling long 24 miles left me "hangry"!!!! I found myself reaching for pretzels, chips, processed bars, or cereal as snacks between meals or before bed. I knew this wasn't ideal, but I was hungry ALL THE TIME!!

Fast forward to 4 years ago, insert Elyse and her nutritional wisdom, and I no longer have the uncontrollable and wild cravings for naughty snack foods.

*One of the best gifts I've been given to enhance my running career and overall well-being has been learning to cook.*

Elyse taught me that cooking should be fun and not overwhelming. She showed me how to cook with good fats to add flavor and nourishment. She also told me to stop counting calories and that the only numbers I should be consuming my mind with were the splits on my watch and miles I logged each day. Both of these recommendations were revolutionary ideas to me.

In college, I fell into the misleading trap that all fat was bad. I thought fat would make you fat!! Little did I know, that adding the right fats would make me feel satiated and keep me full longer. Since I started eating this way, it has given me more energy and enables me to recover faster from hard workouts. With more energy comes a boost in enthusiasm for my training and racing. Winner, winner, chicken dinner!!

Since adding more fat and whole foods into my diet, my racing weight now comes naturally—without counting calories. Hallelujah!!!! I used to stress about getting down to my ideal racing weight in the weeks leading up to a major race.

This year I turned 36, which is getting up there in the elite world, and I truly believe changing my diet has enabled me to extend my career. In the past year, I set multiple PRs, ran in my 4th Olympics, and became the first US woman in 40 years to win the NYC Marathon.

I'm running stronger than ever before. My wish for everyone is that you feel this way, too. Unburden and indulge yourself in our delicious recipes and set audacious goals that will fuel your soul!

*Shalane*

# ELYSE'S REAL FOOD STORY

I started running competitively in 7th grade, and for 15 years I suffered from athletic amenorrhea (the absence of menstruation). Doctors told me I would have trouble getting pregnant someday and prescribed artificial hormones. Not one doctor ever suggested that I change my diet.

When I turned 30, I had the chance to work abroad in Switzerland, and my diet changed drastically from low-fat yogurt to whole milk yogurt, from bland white meat chicken breasts to whole roasted chicken, from processed spreads to real butter, and from frozen veggie burgers to full-fat grass-fed ground beef.

---

*This indulgent diet that I had learned to label in our country as unhealthy actually made me stronger, happier, and healthier than ever before.*

---

For the first time in my life, I got my period naturally, and I didn't have to give up the sport that I loved. My time in Europe taught me that food should be celebrated and enjoyed. I discovered a passion for cooking and was eager to learn more about nutrition. The experience was so life-changing that I left behind a successful marketing career and moved to NYC to study culinary nutrition at the Natural Gourmet Institute.

When I finished school and reunited with my husband in Portland, we were ready to start a family. To our sheer delight, we got pregnant our first month trying. The joy my daughter, Lily, brought into our life inspired me to take the plunge and follow my dream of writing *Run Fast. Eat Slow.* I knew my story could help thousands of women.

And it gets better. Lily started asking for a sibling when she turned 2, but I was busy in the midst of our book tour. My husband and

I decided to wait to start trying for a second kid until I started writing this second book. I wanted to have at least 9 months to complete the manuscript before adding in the chaos of a newborn. Let's just say we jumped the gun over the Christmas holidays, convinced it couldn't possibly happen so quickly again. To our complete surprise (and honestly a few stressed tears), we again got pregnant on the first go, a true testament to this way of eating. When we got pregnant with numero two, I was running stronger than my college racing days (finally free from stress fractures) and lapping up the endless mountain trails in our new hometown of Bend, Oregon.

I started writing and developing the recipes for this book right away, since I was now on a time crunch. It's very fitting that I was pregnant the entire time while cooking up book two and Shalane was in serious training mode in preparation for the NYC Marathon—as we were both hungry for new recipes. The meals we developed kept us both energized while working long hours (Shalane on the roads in Mammoth and me in the kitchen in Bend) and enabled us both to achieve our very different goals (Shalane winning a major marathon, me having another healthy pregnancy). I completed the manuscript just days before our adorable son, Rylan, was born on September 22, 2017.

I continue to depend on the recipes within these pages to keep me nourished through the demands of nursing and sleepless nights.

Motherhood is the most rewarding accomplishment of my life. I'm so grateful to have this opportunity to help other women nourish their bodies for the long run.

*Elyse*

*Elyse, 38-weeks pregnant, with husband, Andy Hughes, and 3-year old daughter, Lily, in their backyard in Bend, Oregon.*

# 1 | THE RUN FAST EAT SLOW WAY

*"Healthy eating isn't just kale juice, but also a juicy burger."*

**—ELYSE**

Figuring out how to optimally nourish your body for an active, happy, and healthy life is surprisingly challenging. We live in a culture that both celebrates food and fears it. We know we should eat better, but health food has a reputation of being bland and boring. Nutrition science and the media are constantly fluctuating on what's good versus bad for us. On top of all this, we are just too busy to take the time to cook nourishing meals.

Unfortunately, the bombardment of misinformation around healthy eating has led to an epidemic of disordered eating habits among young athletes. "While disordered eating does not necessarily mean an athlete has an eating disorder (i.e., anorexia nervosa), there is a huge overlap. Many athletes are often unaware of just how many calories they require for their high level of activity. Other athletes may adopt a special diet in hopes of improving their performance, yet not make up the calories that are missing when specific foods are being eliminated," says Jennifer Carlson, MD, who has extensive experience treating amenorrhea and the female athlete triad (disordered eating, amenorrhea, and low bone density) at Stanford University (read our complete interview with Dr. Carlson on page 30). Restrictive fad diets can easily spiral out of control, leading to an unhealthy relationship with food and malnourishment. In fact, in a study of Division 1 NCAA athletes, over one-third of female athletes showed tendencies that put them at risk for anorexia nervosa (nationaleatingdisorders.org).

Even seemingly healthy eaters are often undernourished. Exact statistics are unknown, but experts estimate more than half of female endurance athletes have experienced athletic amenorrhea, with some studies concluding it affects upward of 65 percent of collegiate distance runners. Athletic amenorrhea, also called secondary or hypothalamic amenorrhea, is the absence of menstruation directly related to an energy deficiency. When the body isn't getting enough high-quality fuel, it begins to shut down systems that aren't necessary for survival, and the female reproductive system is one of the first to go.

In the short term, poor nutrition puts athletes at an increased risk of injuries, stress fractures, anemia, fatigue, low immunity, irritability, poor concentration, and more. The long-term repercussions include low bone density, hormone imbalances, decreased metabolism, infertility, chronic diseases, cardiovascular risks, and depression.

In this chapter, we'll explain how to eat healthy without counting calories, why you should ignore the latest diet trends, and how to get back in tune with listening to your body's hunger signals. We'll debunk the myth around fat (bring on the butter!). And we'll teach you how to celebrate real food for the wealth of benefits it provides for both your body and mind.

"The sheer novelty and glamor of the Western diet, with its 17 thousand new food products every year and the marketing power–32 billion dollars a year–used to sell us those products, has overwhelmed the force of tradition and left us where we now find ourselves: relying on science and journalism and government and marketing to help us decide what to eat."

–**MICHAEL POLLAN,**
IN DEFENSE OF FOOD:
AN EATER'S MANIFESTO

"Exercise is enormously beneficial for the mind and body, but can be a detriment to overall health if taken to the extreme. Muscles and bones need both rest and considerable fuel for the tissue regeneration that leads to maximum athletic performance. 'Too much of a good thing' can leave young, competitive athletes weak and—ironically—unhealthy vs. physically fit. Sufficient calories and balanced nutritional intake is essential to long-term engagement in the sport."

**–CATHERINE M. GORDON, MD, MSC,**
LEADING RESEARCHER AND CLINICAL EXPERT
ON HYPOTHALAMIC AMENORRHEA

## DIETING DOES NOT WORK

Restrictive diets can be pretty enticing with all their promises for weight loss, six-pack abs, and eternal beauty. It's not surprising that we easily fall victim to the latest diet trend. The $64 billion weight loss industry is working hard in every media space to get our attention, which can make grocery shopping a confusing, panic-inducing activity.

But the truth is dieting does not work and leads to an unhealthy relationship with food. In the long term most dieters regain the weight lost plus a few new pounds.

There are many compelling reasons why dieting does not work. For starters, it's counterproductive to how your body functions. The body is constantly working hard to maintain balance, and when we restrict calories our metabolism outsmarts us and slows down. The body produces stress hormones in response to less nutrition, and these hormones signal cells to store up reserves resulting in weight gain.

Dieting also leads to thinking about food around the clock, which doesn't help keep hunger signals at bay. The mind wants what it can't have. A month without chocolate can lead to binge eating an entire box of cookies, which can lead to negative feelings and anxiety around food.

Additionally, restricting healthy fats and complex carbs leads to an energy deficiency, which causes sugar cravings. Our bodies end up wanting the quickest fuel source possible, which are simple sugars from refined carbs. And sugar is one of the leading culprits of weight gain.

Lastly, dieting is simply no fun. Healthy eating should not be restrictive, tiresome, or uninspiring. Nor should healthy eating become obsessive. Food should be celebrated—it nourishes our minds, bodies, and souls. The recipes within will help you indulge in real food with confidence.

## COUNT SPLITS, NOT CALORIES

*"In the past I would feel a burden with my diet. I worried about whether I was eating the right foods and how it would affect my performance. I now focus my energy on the quality of food instead of measuring quantities. I spend enough time counting miles and calculating splits on the track. I don't need to bring math into the kitchen, too."*

**–SHALANE**

After our first cookbook launched, we received emails from runners who were upset that we didn't provide calorie counts and carb, fat, and protein measurements. Despite the complaints, we received more emails from happy fans relieved to eat without numbers dictating their appetites. For our second cookbook, we stand by our belief that calorie counts have no place in the kitchen. When you're slicing and dicing real food, what really matters is taste and satisfaction.

A calorie is a unit of measure based on estimates. Think back to science class. Do you know what a calorie actually measures? We had to check Wikipedia ourselves. It's defined as "the approximate amount of energy needed to raise the temperature of 1 gram of water by 1 degree Celsius at a pressure of one atmosphere." Huh?! In 1824, a scientist calculated the number of calories in a gram of fat, protein, and carbohydrate.

These rough calculations from nearly 200 years ago are still used to determine the calories listed on every single packaged food.

We now know that everyone burns a calorie differently. Digestion and metabolism are intricate processes that vary greatly from person to person. How much energy one person extracts from a hunk of cheese is different from the next person. Different foods are also burned differently. A calorie from an almond does not provide equivalent energy as a calorie from a Twizzler. Complex stuff!

Additionally, people who count calories depend on packaged foods, since these foods make it easy to calculate numbers. But packaged foods are the very foods that cause weight gain. Whole foods, without the pretty packages and fancy numbers, leave us better nourished, more satisfied, and less likely to overeat.

Instead of following rules, we want to teach you to get back in tune with listening to your body's hunger signals. First, trust that your body knows best. It can be hard to listen to hunger cues if you're constantly eating while on the run or in front of the TV. Turn off electronics so you can eat mindfully. Enjoy your meals with friends and family. Slow down and chew your food so your stomach has time to register how much you're consuming (Eat Slow!). And most important, everything you eat should taste amazing so that you feel satisfied at the end of a meal. That leads us to our next point. Bring on the fat.

# BIG FAT MYTH

*"Maybe you need more butter in your life."*
**–ELYSE**

For years we were told to eat less fat because it was believed to cause weight gain and high cholesterol. The reality is whole food fats are essential for maintaining a healthy weight and help your body produce good (HDL) cholesterol. Despite all the nutrition science out there that debunks the notion that fat is bad, many runners still have an ingrained fear of fat.

While on our book tour, we often got asked, "I'm not running 100 miles per week like Shalane, so how can I eat like her?" Whether you're a beginner training for your first 5K and trying to shed a few pounds or an elite athlete training for a marathon, you still need healthy fats in your life.

In the 1970s, Americans developed a fear of fat after the government came together with major food companies to declare that saturated fat causes heart disease. Soon after, the packaged foods industry boomed with aisles of low-fat and fat-free products. Not surprisingly, during this "fat-free" era, Americans gained weight at an alarming rate.

Turns out a diet rich in whole food fats (even saturated fat) is essential for a healthy metabolism, balanced hormones, and satiation—all of which prevent weight gain.

Nourishing fats are essential for brain function. Studies show that fat helps prevent depression, balances our emotions, and improves concentration. A high-fat diet is especially important for pregnant and nursing women, and for babies and young children to help with brain development.

Fat-soluble vitamins like A, D, E, and K can't be digested without fat in our diets. Fat helps transport these essential nutrients to every system in our body.

Additionally, fat is one of the best sources of usable energy for endurance endeavors. It provides balanced energy instead of a sugar high and crash. Medium-chain fatty acids (found in coconut oil, butter, and whole milk yogurt) are especially efficient, since they're metabolized fast.

We're even convinced that butter is more nourishing for an athlete than kale! Can't believe it? Hear us out:

>> High-quality butter (organic or local, grass-fed, cultured) is incredibly nutrient-dense, providing vitamins A, D, and E. Vitamin A is essential to a healthy cardiovascular system.

>> Butter is antioxidant-rich—move over pomegranates and blueberries.

>> Grass-fed butter is rich in conjugated linoleic acid (CLA), a fatty acid proven to help your body repair its hard-working muscles. Athletes often obsess over protein, but protein isn't the only essential macronutrient.

>> Butter has anti-inflammatory and antimicrobial properties.

So does butter raise your cholesterol? Numerous studies show likely not. Cholesterol-rich whole foods are essential to help our body repair its 6 trillion cell membranes (cell walls are made out of cholesterol). Cholesterol is used to manufacture essential hormones, and you need good (real food) cholesterol to balance out the bad stuff.

This doesn't mean you should go chomp on an entire stick of butter. But it does mean you should enjoy your kale sautéed in butter (see Miso Fast Greens, page 167), and don't be afraid to add a smear of butter to your toast, broccoli, or steak. If you're following a vegan diet, extra-virgin olive oil, virgin coconut oil, and avocados are great alternatives.

Not all fats are created equal. It's still important to limit consumption of cheap vegetable oils like canola, soybean, and safflower oils, which are found in most packaged foods. Refined vegetable oil is highly inflammatory and high in trans fats, which can raise bad (LDL) cholesterol. Fat also stores toxins and chemicals, so when buying high-fat foods organic is the way to go. Studies show nutrients are much lower in factory-farmed, grain-fed meat, and the good fatty acids are higher in grass-fed meat (plus pasture-raised tastes significantly better).

Butter is just one example of many fun fats to introduce into your culinary endeavors. Variety is best. Here are our favorite real food fats that we use frequently in the recipes within these pages:

>> Grass-fed cultured butter

>> Nuts, seeds, nut butter

>> Extra-virgin olive oil

>> Virgin coconut oil

>> Avocados (and cold-pressed, unrefined avocado oil)

>> Pasture-raised eggs (eat the yolk!)

>> Grass-fed red meat (beef and bison)

>> Organic dark meat chicken

>> Wild salmon

>> Canned sardines in olive oil

>> Organic, plain, whole milk yogurt

>> Aged cheeses and goat cheese

# REAL FOOD FOR THE WIN

---

*"You are imperfect, permanently and inevitably flawed. And you are beautiful."*

**–AMY BLOOM**

---

In our first cookbook, *Run Fast. Eat Slow.: Nourishing Recipes for Athletes*, we talk in detail about how we define "real food" and what ingredients we keep stocked in our pantries and fridge. If you haven't read those chapters lately, they're worth checking out; here's a brief review.

"Real foods" are minimally processed ingredients that are close to their natural, whole food form. This means they look like they came from the land and not from a shiny, crinkly package.

While foods like plain yogurt, aged cheese, nut butter, and extra-virgin olive oil are processed, we still consider these to be whole foods, since they have minimal alterations and a short ingredient list. If your great-grandmother ate the food, it's probably a safe bet for you too.

The foods that are staples in our diet include whole grains, beans, cultured dairy, grass-fed eggs and meat, wild fish, seasonal vegetables and fruit, nuts, seeds, and more. We eat a varied diet to ensure we're getting the full spectrum of micronutrients.

This doesn't mean we eat strictly whole foods all the time, and you shouldn't either.

Stressing that everything you put in your body is organic or whole can easily spiral out of control into obsessive eating habits. If you love ice cream, go ahead and enjoy a bowl. There's barely a day that goes by in Elyse's home where there isn't a baguette or bowl of tortilla chips on the table to go with dinner. And Shalane wouldn't survive without her coffee creamer or favorite dark chocolate bars. Fill up on nourishing, wholesome foods, enjoy favorite treats in moderation, spend more time in the kitchen, and you'll be on the right path.

Read inspiring real food transformation stories from our fans starting on page 240.

# EPIDEMIC OF DISORDERED EATING HABITS

## AN INTERVIEW WITH JENNIFER CARLSON, MD

We caught up with Dr. Jennifer Carlson, clinical associate professor of adolescent medicine at the Stanford University School of Medicine, and a leading researcher in the treatment of amenorrhea and the female athlete triad, to learn more about the prevalence of harmful energy deficiencies in athletes. We spoke to her specifically about the issues that develop for female athletes, but it should be noted that male endurance athletes are also prone to health issues related to undernourishment and can equally benefit from the advice within *Run Fast. Cook Fast. Eat Slow.*

---

**Q** WHAT PERCENTAGE OF YOUNG COMPETITIVE RUNNERS DO YOU THINK SUFFER FROM ATHLETIC AMENORRHEA?

>> The numbers really vary between different studies and may reflect a number of factors: which athletes are being studied, how the questions are being asked, and whether a study is looking at amenorrhea or the range of menstrual dysfunction that may affect an athlete. In the literature, anywhere from 3 to 65 percent of female athletes are reported to be amenorrheic, though rates of other types of menstrual irregularities (oligomenorrhea, luteal phase deficiency) are even higher. In my clinic, this is an extremely common concern and the one that often triggers an athlete to visit her physician for further evaluation.

**Q** FROM YOUR LATEST RESEARCH, WHAT IS THE LEADING CAUSE OF THE ABSENCE OF MENSTRUATION IN SO MANY FEMALE ATHLETES?

>> Though there are many different reasons that an athlete (just as any woman) can have an absence of menstruation, the leading cause in athletes is an energy imbalance leading to low estrogen (estradiol) levels. If an athlete is not eating enough calories to compensate for her baseline metabolic needs as well as the increased amount of calories burned in exercise (particularly for runners), then she will have an overall negative energy balance. This negative energy balance results in the suppression of the hormones that control menstruation. With an estrogen level that is too low, periods will not occur regularly, and an athlete will be at risk for some of the other medical complications associated with low estrogen levels (like muscle and bone injuries and low bone mineral density).

## Q HOW COMMON ARE DISORDERED EATING HABITS AMONG HIGH SCHOOL AND COLLEGE ATHLETES?

>> Disordered eating is extremely common among high school and college athletes. While disordered eating does not necessarily mean an athlete has an eating disorder (i.e., anorexia nervosa), there is a huge overlap. Many athletes are often unaware of just how many calories they require for their high level of activity. Other athletes may adopt a special diet in hopes of improving their performance, yet not make up the calories that are missing when specific foods are being eliminated. I see many athletes who are eating large volumes of food, but the calorie and nutrient content is way too low to meet their energy needs.

## Q WHAT IS CAUSING THIS EPIDEMIC OF UNDERNOURISHED ATHLETES AND EATING DISORDERS?

>> There are likely several reasons contributing to the link of athletes and eating disorders. Athletics, in general, are becoming more competitive in youth, often specializing in a sport at incredibly young ages. There is a lot of dietary advice being given to athletes at all levels that may not reflect the increased needs of the growing and developing bodies of adolescents and young adults; it is a setup for undernourished athletes. Our food culture also touts many different food fads that may not be appropriate for athletes with high caloric needs. For example, if an athlete chooses to become vegan and gluten-free, it is going to be a time-consuming process to get in the volume of food that she will require for her energy needs and nutrient balance. Eating disorders are slowly losing the stigma associated with them, and people are starting to speak out about their struggles. With more awareness, individuals who may not have discussed their struggles in the past may be feeling more supported to do so now.

## Q WHAT CAN BE DONE TO HELP PREVENT EATING DISORDERS AMONG YOUNG RUNNERS?

>> Education about energy needs and balance in intake are critical components to maintaining good health for an athlete. Athletes and all the people who support athletes (parents, family, coaches, trainers, teammates) need to be educated about the importance of appropriate nutrition and the signs of an energy imbalance. Athletes need to be aware that missing a period during their season should not be considered a normal, possibly convenient, side effect of training. Rather, it is a sign that one's body is not functioning normally and is at increased risk of short- and long-term complications.

For more help on this topic, check out the National Eating Disorder Association (NEDA) at nationaleatingdisorders.org. The website is full of resources, including a free online tool kit for athletes (and coaches). The Female Athlete Triad Coalition (femaleathletetriad.org) is also a great resource for athletes and coaches.

# 2 | JUMP-START YOUR KITCHEN

*"Outside of running more miles, the single greatest thing athletes can do to improve their performance (and their long-term health and happiness) is to learn to cook."*

**—ELYSE**

**W**e heard ya loud and clear: Your biggest obstacle to cooking incredible, nourishing meals from scratch is time and money. We've got your back. In this chapter we'll share our tried-and-true tricks for getting dinner on the table pronto. We'll tell you which kitchen tools are must-haves, explain how to meal plan like a champ, and share our best budget-saving tips.

We carefully crafted every recipe in this book to save you time in the kitchen. We eliminated any ingredients that weren't completely necessary. We broke traditional techniques to compress steps. We eliminated unnecessary dishes—all while ensuring each recipe turns out delicious time after time.

While we love cooking, we too don't want to spend all day in the kitchen. We hope these tips and our simple recipes will enable you to spend more time pursuing your favorite athletic endeavors and less time stressing about what's for breakfast, lunch, and dinner.

# TIME-SAVING TOOLS

Here are a few of our favorite time-saving kitchen gadgets.

---

## >> INSTANT POT
## (ELECTRIC PRESSURE COOKER)

This impressive machine pretty much does it all. It's a combination slow cooker and pressure cooker and even has a sauté setting. It's an investment and takes up considerable cabinet space, but you'll find yourself using it so frequently that you'll probably end up leaving it out on your counter. We use it to cook rice, beans, grains, sweet potatoes, beets, bone broth, soups, and perfect hard-boiled eggs.

## >> RICE COOKER

If you aren't quite ready to take on a pressure cooker (see above), then we'd recommend getting a simple rice cooker—especially if rice bowls make a weekly appearance in your home like they do in ours (see Power Bowls, page 122).

## >> CHEF'S KNIFE

A high-quality 8-inch classic chef's knife is worth its weight in gold. The recipes in this book require considerable chopping, since we love fresh produce. A sharp knife will save you serious time. We also highly recommend taking a knife skills class. A few basic skills will give you confidence (and save your fingers).

## >> QUALITY POTS AND PANS

High-quality pots and pans conduct heat better, which means your food will cook more evenly and quicker than in low-quality cookware. Look for heavy-bottomed pots and pans made from stainless steel and/or copper. We also couldn't live without our well-seasoned cast-iron skillet (the more you use it, the better it gets).

## >> DUTCH/FRENCH OVEN

We're obsessed with our 7-quart Le Creuset Signature French Oven. The large size is ideal for making double batches of soup, stews, and sauces. The cast-iron conducts heat incredibly well to help you get dinner on the table faster (plus it doubles as a beautiful serving dish). Its surface is nonstick, easy to clean, and free of chemicals. It is expensive but will last a lifetime.

## >> LARGE CUTTING BOARD

Invest in a solid wooden cutting board in a large size so that you can chop every last veggie in one swoop. Lay a dishtowel under your board to keep it from sliding while chopping.

## >> GLASS JARS AND CONTAINERS

Stock up on glass jars and glass canisters in a variety of sizes to store grains, nuts, seeds, and more. They're also great for shaking up salad dressing and packing a smoothie to go. Our favorite is freezer-safe 1½ pint wide-mouthed Ball jars and OXO Smart Seal glass containers. Not all glass jars are freezer safe, so check the package.

## >> HIGH-SPEED BLENDER

Professional-quality blenders are expensive but worth it, since they can also do the work of a food processor. We use our Vitamix on a near daily basis to make smoothies, creamy soups, pesto, hummus, sauces, nut butter, nut milk, and energy bars and to finely chop veggies.

## >> GARLIC PRESS

Shalane's least favorite prep work is mincing garlic. She loves her garlic press, and it certainly is a handy gadget.

# ELYSE'S TOP TIME-SAVING TIPS

I'll be the first to admit—cooking takes serious time and effort. If you want to put nourishing meals on your table every day, you just might have to get up earlier in the morning, give up your nightly Netflix binge, or—gasp!—spend less time on your phone.

But once you start eating right, you'll gain a new level of energy that makes you much more productive. At the end of the day, fueling your body with wholesome, real food will make you faster at everything else in your life, not just running.

If Shalane can whip up rice bowls with roasted veggies, burgers, and homemade sauce after a 20-mile training run, you too can dig deep and find the energy to get into the kitchen. Let's get started!

**1** >> **MEAL PLAN LIKE YOU PLAN YOUR TRAINING** This is one of the hardest tips to turn into a habit, but it will save you tons of time. By planning out your meals for the week, you can do one big grocery run. Fewer trips to the store will also save you money, since you can plan meals back-to-back that make use of the same ingredients. You'll also be less likely to end up at a takeout joint if your fridge is well stocked. Organize your grocery list by section of the store so that you don't feel overwhelmed while navigating the endless aisles. See "Meal Planning" on page 41 for more on this.

**2** >> **COOK IN BULK** Learn to cook family favorite recipes in larger batches especially for dishes that freeze well (see freezer tips on page 38). Any time I'm making a sauce or soup, I double the recipe. Also get in the habit of prepping ingredients that you can use for multiple dishes. For example, wash and chop veggies for several days all in one go and store in airtight containers. Cook enough rice or quinoa for multiple dinners. Grill or roast extra veggies to serve as a side dish one night and then toss into pasta or rice bowls the next night.

**3** >> **YOUR FREEZER IS YOUR BFF** Many sauces and dishes freeze incredibly well. Portion leftovers into individual containers and freeze for work, school lunches, or future dinners. Freeze leftover baked goods into snack-size bags and grab a bag on your way out the door; it will be thawed by snack time. Having treats packed in healthy serving sizes also helps with portion control. You'll be less tempted to eat the entire batch of cookies if you've taken the time to individually wrap and freeze them.

**4** >> **DEDICATE ONE AFTERNOON** Turn up the music, open a bottle of vino, download a favorite podcast, block out your calendar. Do whatever it takes to dedicate one afternoon per week for meal prep. You'll be a lot less likely to pick up a burrito on the way home from practice if you have the quinoa and sauce already made and all you need to do is sauté some chicken and veggies. See "5 Things to Make Every Week" on page 41. Follow my weekly meal prep on Instagram @elysekopecky.

**5** **>> START WITH THE BEST INGREDIENTS**
Fresh, high-quality ingredients require less work in the kitchen to transform into deliciousness. There is a huge difference in taste between produce that has been shipped from halfway around the world and produce grown locally. Local produce is picked at the peak of freshness and delivered to you before the nutrients and flavors begin to degrade. Organic or local meat, eggs, and dairy products are also more nutritious. Food from family farms is often more expensive, but the quality is so much better. Read "Buy Organic Strategically" under "Budget Tips" on page 39.

**6** **>> EMBRACE CREATIVE LEFTOVERS**
Many of the main dishes in this book can be transformed into multiple dinners. Our favorite way to use up leftovers is on top of rice bowls or salads (see Power Bowls, page 122). We have yet to find a meat or veggie that isn't happy sitting atop a bowl of fluffy rice with a drizzle of sauce. Don't toss out anything. Little bits of leftovers can be transformed into flavorful pizza toppings, used as ingredients for a scramble, or tossed into pasta. If you're cooking for a family, scale recipes up to ensure you have leftovers (see tip #2).

**7** **>> ENLIST YOUR TRIBE** Those who cook together, stick together! Cooking is a lot of fun when you do it with friends or family. If you're a college student, enlist your roommates to take turns cooking a meal for the whole house. If you're single and working, start a monthly cooking club where everyone brings a double batch of a homemade freezer-friendly meal to swap. If you're a parent, get your kids into the kitchen. Kids are a lot more likely to taste a new dish if they've helped prepare it.

**8** **>> READ THE RECIPE AND PREP THE INGREDIENTS** Before you dive into step one of a recipe, it's critical to read the entire recipe. Knowing the steps in advance will save you time and prevent any unwanted surprises (like realizing an hour before dinner that an ingredient needs to soak overnight). You'll also be able to work much faster if you have all the ingredients in front of you and prepped before you begin. In our recipes, vegetable preparation instructions appear within the ingredient list, not within the steps.

**9** **>> KEEP BASICS STOCKED** Stock your pantry with all the basics like flours, grains, beans, pasta, vinegars, oils, sweeteners, nuts, seeds, and seasonings and you'll save time at the grocery store. This enables you to avoid getting lost in the endless aisles of packaged foods when you're just running in to grab fresh ingredients for dinner. You'll be able to stick to the outer perimeter of the grocery store, which is where all the whole foods are stocked. If you need more guidance, check out the chapter on how to stock your pantry in our first cookbook.

**10** **>> MULTITASK LIKE A CHEF**
Once you get the hang of cooking, you'll discover it's fun to channel your inner chef and manage multiple pots on the stove at the same time. For example, while the soup simmers, cook hard-boiled eggs or quinoa for lunch the next day. Waiting for the oven to preheat? Whirl together a smoothie for breakfast. Your oven can multitask, too. While the chicken bakes, throw in a couple of sweet potatoes or beets on the top shelf of the oven for future dinners, or, when you bake cookies, roast a tray of nuts. Just be sure to set multiple kitchen timers so you can keep track of everything!

# BUDGET TIPS

We'll tell you straight up: Eating healthy is expensive. But you're worth it. Think of it in terms of an investment in your future self.

Buying healthy food now will save you serious dough in the future on medical costs for issues that might have been avoidable. For example, the right nutrition can prevent common running injuries like stress fractures. X-rays and a few physical therapy sessions are way more expensive than a month's worth of high-quality groceries.

Here's a shocking statistic: Americans spend less of their income on groceries than people do in any other country in the world. According to the US Department of Agriculture, we spend just 6.4 percent of our household income on food. We have come to expect food to be cheap, but inexpensive food is nutrition-less and directly linked to a wide range of health issues.

**1 >> SHOP SEASONALLY** Sure, you can buy strawberries and tomatoes in the dead of winter, but they'll be flavorless and cost you a fortune compared to in-season produce. Out-of-season produce is grown in greenhouses or shipped from halfway around the world. Produce that travels great distances is more expensive and less nutritious, since it's picked before it has the chance to ripen.

**2 >> BEELINE FOR THE BULK BINS** Dry goods like flours, whole grains, beans, nuts, seeds, and dried fruit are often much cheaper when you buy them from the bulk bins. These foods have a long shelf life, and if stored properly, they'll stay fresh for months (invest in a set of large glass canisters). Many grocery stores also sell spices by weight, so you can bag the exact quantity that you need for significantly less (spices lose flavor quickly, so only buy what you'll use up in a few months).

**3 >> SIGN UP FOR A CSA** If you're committed to cooking and eating more veggies, join a CSA (community-supported agriculture) to receive a weekly delivery of seasonal, local produce. The veggies will be significantly more flavorful, fresh, and nutritious than anything you'll find at the grocery store and less expensive than the farmers' market.

**4 >> LEVERAGE YOUR FREEZER** Your freezer can help save you moola if you keep it organized and ensure that foods are well labeled. Often things that go into the freezer never come back out, so labeling everything and keeping a running tally of what's hiding in there can help. See tip #3 under "Elyse's Top Time-Saving Tips" on page 36.

In Elyse's freezer you'll find a drawer dedicated to meat bought in bulk directly from local farmers, a shelf dedicated to ingredients for smoothies (you can rescue fruits and veggies that are about to go bad by popping them into the freezer), a space dedicated to wholesome, baked goods individually wrapped for convenience, and a shelf dedicated to homemade sauces, broth, and cooked beans and grains. Elyse also freezes soups and stews into individual serving containers for speedy work lunches. You'll have less temptation to buy lunch or order takeout when you have meals at the ready for "hangry" days.

**5** >> **BUY ORGANIC STRATEGICALLY** Don't stress at the store. Not everything you buy has to be organic. If you're on a budget, Google "Dirty Dozen" and "Clean Fifteen" for a list of the most pesticide- and least pesticide-ridden produce. As a rule of thumb, anything with a thick skin that you toss like oranges and melons is safe to buy conventional. The foods we are always willing to pay organic (or local) prices for include produce, dairy, meat, and eggs. When we're shopping at the farmers' market, we don't stress about buying only organic. Small farmers can't always afford organic certification, but their farming practices are commendable.

**6** >> **PACK YOUR LUNCH** You can save some serious money if you start taking your lunch to school or work. Plus, homemade lunches are guaranteed to leave you feeling more nourished and energized, so you'll be less likely to reach for a $5 afternoon latte. Skip highly processed turkey sandwiches and instead opt for any of the recipes in our Lunch Pail chapter (page 88). These dishes were designed to be packable, since we know you're always on the go.

**7** >> **COOK FROM SCRATCH** Some of the most expensive products at the grocery store are things you can easily make from scratch at home. Skip the expensive ready-made dishes in the deli counter and leave the fancy packaged sauces, dressings, and healthy-*sounding* snack foods behind for real-deal homemade goodness.

**8** >> **STOCK UP ON STAPLES** Now that you're buying a lot less packaged snack foods, you'll have more room in your pantry to stock up on real food staples when they're on sale. Grocery stores are very cost competitive. You'll likely come across major sales on the expensive essentials that we use frequently in this book, such as olive oil, coconut oil, vinegar, fancy whole grains and flours, maple syrup, honey, canned goods, and so on.

**9** >> **LESS MEAT BUT MAKE IT COUNT** A vegetarian dinner of beans (or Crispy Tempeh, page 143), whole grains, and sautéed greens will only set you back a couple of dollars. Meat is expensive but worth eating for its recovery superpowers. If you're on a budget, limit meat to just a few nights per week or opt for less expensive cuts. Chicken thighs, ground beef, and canned sardines are cheap and nutritious. When it comes to meat and seafood, it's better to eat higher quality and less of it. Buy your meat in bulk direct from a local farmer and you'll be set for months.

**10** >> **BRING A LIST** If you're following our time-saving tips and planning out your meals for the week in advance, you'll be able to head to the store with a detailed shopping list. This will prevent you from buying unnecessary items that end up growing mold in the back of the fridge. During the week, jot down in your phone ingredients that are getting low. On your shopping day, write out a complete list with produce on the left side of the page and other ingredients on the right side of the page. As you shop, check off what's in your cart by simply making a little tear mark on the paper. Or you could download a fancy grocery app, but we found this system to be faster.

## MEAL PLANNING

Block out 30 minutes in your calendar toward the end of every week to plan your meals for the following week. Include weekday breakfasts that can be repeated to save you time, dinners that can be transformed into lunches, and weekly staples. Not every dinner needs to be planned in advance, as some of the best meals come together at the last minute using up an assortment of leftovers. Having at least 3 main meals with the ingredients stocked in your fridge will save you from last-minute panic and rushed trips to the grocery store. Also, it's okay to repeat family favorites every week. For example, Elyse's family plans rice bowl night (see Power Bowls, page 122) and a pizza night every week and just varies the toppings based on leftovers on hand.

### 5 THINGS TO MAKE EVERY WEEK

Busy working moms know firsthand that dinner needs to come together pronto. This prevents the kids from filling up on snacks and helps to keep bedtime on track. Having the basics prepped in advance (see tip #4 on page 36) enables you to get dinner on the table in 30 minutes or less.

When her family isn't off on a camping adventure, Elyse spends Sunday afternoons in the kitchen prepping for the week. Here are the staples she makes every week. If you can manage three of the below, you're a star; manage all five and you're a rock star.

1. Cook a big batch of wholesome grains like rice, farro, or quinoa to be used for breakfast (Peaches and Molasses Quinoa Bowl, page 69), lunch (DIY Grain Salad, page 95), and/or dinner (Power Bowls, page 122).

2. Make a homemade sauce and/or dressing (Chapter 7, page 170).

3. Roast a tray of veggies (Sunday Sweet Potatoes, page 161; Roasted Cauliflower and Potatoes, page 162; Simply Roasted Vegetables, page 159).

4. Make a soup (winter) or a hearty grain salad (summer) (DIY Grain Salad, page 95; Kale and Edamame Orange Miso Salad, page 96; Chicken Cannellini Soup, page 116; Superfoods Soup, page 112).

5. Prep simple snacks like hummus and veggies, hard-boiled eggs, bags of trail mix) or bake a wholesome treat (Superhero Muffins, page 60; Molasses Granola Bars, page 229).

### EATING ON THE GO

We know your life is too busy to sit down for every meal. And if you're like us, "hangry" symptoms can come on fast and furious. Plan ahead and make it a habit to bring along your own wholesome food to work, school, practice, and so on. Always carry snacks and water to prevent the temptation to grab sugary packaged foods (even healthy-sounding protein bars are loaded with refined sweeteners).

Many of the recipes in this book were designed to be packable. The smoothies, soups, and salads can be packed in wide-mouthed glass jars. The wholesome baked treats and homemade energy bars can be wrapped individually for grab-n-go convenience. The Power Snacks chapters are full of both savory and sweet energizing snacks. The Race Ready chapter includes homemade race-day fuel and all-natural sports drinks.

# SHALANE'S FAVORITES WHILE TRAINING FOR THE NYC MARATHON

In 2017 Shalane made history by becoming the first US woman in 40 years to win the TCS New York City Marathon. Here are the meals she dished out in her buildup to achieving this audacious lifelong goal.

# SHALANE'S SAMPLE MEAL PLAN: *SPRING/SUMMER*

The seasonal meal plans below feature breakfasts, lunches, dinners, and snacks that are easy to repurpose into multiple meals. These meal plans include a lot of variety to maximize your range of nutrients. The dishes are balanced to ensure you're getting enough protein, fat, and complex carbs. If you're cooking solo, you'll have a lot more leftovers, so space these meals out.

| | SUNDAY | MONDAY | TUESDAY |
|---|---|---|---|
| **BREAKFAST** | >> Oatmeal Banana Pancakes *(page 80)* with nut butter<br>>> sliced banana<br>>> coffee with cream | >> Rad Raspberry Beet Smoothie Bowl *(page 56)*<br>>> toast with butter<br>>> coffee with cream | >> leftover pancakes with banana<br>>> scrambled eggs<br>>> coffee with cream |
| **LUNCH** | >> Thai Quinoa Salad *(page 90)* topped with leftover chicken | >> Thai Quinoa Salad *(page 90)*<br>>> hard-boiled egg | >> Thai Quinoa Salad *(page 90)*<br>>> bakery bread with butter |
| **SNACK** | >> Savory Pretzel Granola *(page 191)*<br>>> banana<br>>> Shalane's Natural Sports Drink *(page 233)* | >> Chocolate Coconut Cashew Energy Bar *(page 225)*<br>>> peach | >> Sweet Potato Hummus *(page 195)* and tortilla chips<br>>> berries |
| **DINNER** | >> Miso Butter Salmon *(page 155)*<br>>> Sunday Sweet Potatoes *(page 161)*<br>>> simple salad | >> Rice bowl with leftover salmon<br>>> sweet potatoes<br>>> Miso Fast Greens *(page 167)* | >> Crispy Tempeh *(page 143)* with leftover rice and greens<br>>> Coconut Curry Sauce |
| **SNACK** | >> Lemon Hazelnut Cookie *(page 204)*<br>>> herbal tea | >> whole milk yogurt with Honey Cardamom Granola *(page 64)*<br>>> herbal tea | >> Lemon Hazelnut Cookie *(page 204)*<br>>> herbal tea |

These meal plans include some of Shalane's favorite dishes that fueled her training while preparing for her historic win at the 2017 NYC Marathon.

*In a typical week, Shalane will rely on leftovers more often. The below includes more variety to showcase many favorites.*

| WEDNESDAY | THURSDAY | FRIDAY | SATURDAY |
|---|---|---|---|
| >> Avocado Toast *(page 85)* with leftover greens and fried egg<br>>> berries<br>>> coffee with cream | >> Beet Blueberry Molasses Superhero Muffin *(page 63)*<br>>> Peachy Green Smoothie *(page 58)*<br>>> coffee with cream | >> Peaches and Molasses Quinoa Bowl *(page 69)*<br>>> coffee with cream | >> Spinach and Sausage Fritatta *(page 79)*<br>>> toast with butter<br>>> coffee with cream |
| >> Mediterranean Hummus Wrap *(page 108)*<br>>> Chocolate Peanut Butter Cups *(page 210)* | >> Mediterranean Hummus Wrap *(page 108)*<br>>> fruit salad | >> DIY Grain Salad *(page 95)*<br>>> hard-boiled egg<br>>> leftover soup | >> leftover DIY Grain Salad with leftover hummus on pita |
| >> Savory Pretzel Granola *(page 191)*<br>>> plum<br>>> Lemon Gingerade *(page 230)* | >> Maple Turmeric Nuts *(page 200)*<br>>> banana<br>>> Lemon Gingerade *(page 230)* | >> Sweet Potato Hummus *(page 195)* and carrots<br>>> Anti-Inflammatory Chocolate "Milk" *(page 236)* | >> Chocolate Coconut Cashew Energy Bar *(page 225)*<br>>> peach |
| >> Bonk Burgers *(page 139)*<br>>> Purple Cabbage Slaw *(page 165)*<br>>> Garlicky Guac *(page 177)* | >> Burger Salad Power Bowl *(page 123)*<br>>> Spring Asparagus Soup *(page 119)* | >> Pesto Pasta with Sardines *(page 148)*<br>>> simple green salad | >> Honey Balsamic Grilled Chicken *(page 135)*<br>>> Southwest Salad *(page 98)* |
| >> Strawberry-Rhubarb Chia Parfait *(page 217)*<br>>> herbal tea | >> whole milk yogurt with Honey Cardamom Granola *(page 64)*<br>>> berries<br>>> herbal tea | >> Strawberry-Rhubarb Chia Parfait *(page 217)*<br>>> herbal tea | >> Chocolate Peanut Butter Cups *(page 210)*<br>>> berries<br>>> herbal tea |

# SHALANE'S SAMPLE MEAL PLAN: *FALL/WINTER*

| | SUNDAY | MONDAY | TUESDAY |
|---|---|---|---|
| **BREAKFAST** | >> Wild Rice Pancakes (*page 81*) with fried egg<br>>> avocado<br>>> coffee with cream | >> scrambled eggs with leftover potatoes & cauliflower<br>>> toast with butter<br>>> coffee with cream | >> Apple Pie Steel-Cut Oatmeal (*page 77*)<br>>> coffee with cream |
| **LUNCH** | >> Kale and Edamame Orange Miso Salad (*page 96*)<br>>> Lemon Gingerade (*page 230*) | >> leftover kale salad<br>>> leftover Wild Rice Pancake with cream cheese | >> leftover kale salad topped with leftover chicken or fried egg |
| **SNACK** | >> Molasses Granola Bar (*page 229*)<br>>> apple slices | >> Maple Turmeric Nuts (*page 200*)<br>>> orange<br>>> Shalane's Natural Sports Drink (*page 233*) | >> Molasses Granola Bar (*page 229*)<br>>> apple slices |
| **DINNER** | >> Turkey Trot Meatballs with Marinara (*page 147*)<br>>> Roasted Cauliflower and Potatoes (*page 162*) | >> Power Bowl (*page 122*) with leftover meatballs<br>>> Miso Fast Greens (*page 167*) | >> Superfoods Soup (*page 112*) with Pesto Tuna Melt (*page 107*) |
| **SNACK** | >> Ginger Molasses Cookie (*page 208*)<br>>> herbal tea | >> Chai Cashew Butter (*page 222*) on crackers<br>>> herbal tea | >> Nori Popcorn (*page 198*)<br>>> dried apricots<br>>> herbal tea |

| WEDNESDAY | THURSDAY | FRIDAY | SATURDAY |
|---|---|---|---|
| >> leftover oatmeal<br>>> Can't Beet Me Smoothie *(page 52)*<br>>> coffee with cream | >> Pumpkin Spice Superhero Muffin *(page 62)*<br>>> Immune Boost Smoothie *(page 55)*<br>>> coffee with cream | >> whole milk yogurt with Honey Cardamom Granola *(page 64)*<br>>> apple<br>>> coffee with cream | >> Raceday Oatmeal II *(page 59)*<br>>> banana<br>>> coffee with cream |
| >> Curry Egg Salad wrap *(page 93)*<br>>> simple salad | >> leftover soup<br>>> baguette topped with leftover egg salad | >> Sweet Potato Salad on greens *(page 101)*<br>>> leftover scone | >> leftover Sweet Potato Salad<br>>> hard-boiled egg |
| >> Chai Cashew Butter *(page 222)*<br>>> banana<br>>> Shalane's Natural Sports Drink *(page 233)* | >> Molasses Granola Bar *(page 229)*<br>>> oranges | >> Pumpkin Spice Superhero Muffin *(page 62)*<br>>> pear | >> Pumpkin Spice Superhero Muffin *(page 62)*<br>>> apple slices |
| >> leftover Wild Rice Pancakes topped with cream cheese and smoked salmon<br>>> leftover soup | >> Bison Chili with avocado *(page 120)*<br>>> Apple Cheddar Scone *(page 86)* | >> leftover chili on brown rice with avocado | >> Marathon Bolognese with pasta *(page 144)*<br>>> simple salad |
| >> Nori Popcorn and nuts *(page 198)*<br>>> herbal tea | >> Minute Mug Cake *(page 214)* with whole milk yogurt<br>>> herbal tea | >> Ginger Molasses Cookie *(page 208)*<br>>> herbal tea | >> Minute Mug Cake with whole milk yogurt *(page 216)*<br>>> herbal tea |

## RECIPE ORGANIZATION

The recipes within are organized by time of day to bring you nourishment around the clock. For example, we divided the breakfast chapter into two chapters because if you train in the morning you probably like to have a light, quick bite before you head out the door followed by a hearty "second breakfast."

The **RISE AND RUN** chapter is great for quick weekday breakfasts and the **LONG RUN BRUNCH** chapter is awesome for indulgent meals on the weekend to recover after a serious run. Many of the brunch recipes are also awesome for dinner. Breakfast for dinner—yes, please!

The **LUNCH PAIL** chapter features meals that are easy to pack. These dishes will inspire you to get out of a peanut butter and jelly or turkey sandwich rut. This chapter also includes hearty meal-size salads, which are stellar for lunch or dinner.

The **DINNER BELL** chapter features our go-to, no-fuss, favorite dinner recipes including veg-loaded soups and sides to round out your menu. We give a lot of options within the recipes to inspire you to improvise with seasonal produce. The dishes can be easily repurposed into creative leftovers to save you time and moola. We're especially excited to teach you how to create your own "Power Bowls" (page 122) because they're a versatile weeknight palate pleaser.

### ICON GUIDE
Throughout the recipes we include inspirational tips and tricks to keep you on point.

**Running Tips**

**Time-Saving Tips**

**Nutrition Tips**

**Elite Runner Tips**

The **SAUCY** chapter should not be forgotten. This chapter includes sauces, dressings, and condiments to take your meals from blah to rah-rah-rah.

Lastly, we divided the snacks into **SWEET, SAVORY,** and **RACE READY** chapters because we know your cravings and needs vary depending on your training.

Sprinkled throughout the recipe pages are Shalane's and Elyse's best training tips, motivational quotes, and nutritional wisdom, so you just might want to sit down and read this entire book cover to cover while you munch on Savory Pretzel Granola (page 191) or Nori Popcorn (page 198).

Or just get cooking and you'll discover our top tips along the way. Ready? Set. Go forth into your kitchen!

# 3 | RISE & RUN

*"Every morning in Africa a gazelle wakes
up, it knows it must outrun the fastest lion
or it will be killed. Every morning in Africa
a lion wakes up, it knows it must run faster
than the slowest gazelle, or it will starve.
It doesn't matter whether you're the lion
or a gazelle—when the sun comes up, you'd
better be running."*

**–AUTHOR UNKNOWN**

# CAN'T BEET ME SMOOTHIE 2.0

**FOR TEARING UP THE COMPETITION**

1 small or ½ large cooked beet (see Stopwatch note), peeled

1 cup frozen blueberries

1 frozen banana

1 cup unsweetened almond milk

1 cup coconut water

2 tablespoons unsweetened cocoa powder

1 heaping tablespoon peanut butter

---

If you have a high-speed blender such as a Vitamix, you don't need to cook the beet. Using it raw preserves nutrients, and it will puree completely in the blender. Simply peel and quarter. For rushed mornings, this smoothie can be made the night before. Just stir in the a.m. and sip while you lace up.

We brought back the game-changing Can't Beet Me Smoothie from our first book with a genius twist. We've upped the power and completely changed the flavor by adding in a scoop of anti-oxidant and mineral rich cocoa powder. The deep purple color and rich chocolaty-nutty flavor will make you swoon. When Shalane hosted a high school team cooking party with Makenna, her coach's daughter, the girls went crazy for this smoothie.

Beets are a favorite among elite athletes, since they're packed with nutrients, and studies show they may help improve endurance. This smoothie is also high in essential electrolytes, thanks to the addition of banana and coconut water. **SERVES 2**

---

In a blender, place the beet, blueberries, banana, milk, coconut water, cocoa powder, and peanut butter. Blend on high speed for several minutes until smooth.

### QUICK STEAMED BEETS

Cut unpeeled beets into quarters. Place in a steamer basket in a small pot and fill with just enough water to reach the bottom of the basket (to preserve nutrients you don't want the beets simmering directly in the water). Cover and bring the water to a boil. Reduce the heat to low and simmer for 20 to 25 minutes. Cool, peel, and store in the fridge for up to 5 days.

### ROASTED BEETS

Wrap unpeeled, trimmed beets individually in foil and place on a rimmed baking sheet. Roast in the oven at 400°F for 45 minutes to 1 hour. Beets are done when a butter knife easily pierces through the center of each beet. Cool, peel, and store in the fridge for up to 5 days.

**GLUTEN-FREE // VEGAN**

"Working hard is one thing, but working hard with purpose is what separates the good from the great."

**–THAD MATTA**

# IMMUNE-BOOST SMOOTHIE
## FOR REVVING YOUR RESISTANCE

1 apple, quartered,
core removed

½ frozen banana

2 kale leaves, stems
removed

1 celery stalk, quartered

½ lemon, seeds removed,
peeled

¼ cup parsley leaves

1-inch knob fresh ginger,
peeled, optional

2 cups coconut water

1 cup ice

Add a spoonful of
virgin coconut oil
to the above to help your
body absorb the fat-
soluble vitamins. Coconut
oil is an energizing fat
with natural antimicrobial
properties, making it good
for your immune system.

Intense training or racing can easily leave your immune system
overtaxed and unable to fend off the common cold. This
smoothie will give you the immunity boost you need to get back
on track. And unlike most veggie juices and smoothies, this one
actually tastes good, too.

Besides optimum nutrition, less stress and quality sleep are
vital to making it through the winter months without snot rockets.
Check out Shalane's sleep tips on page 150. **SERVES 2**

In a blender, combine the apple, banana, kale, celery, lemon,
parsley, ginger (if using), coconut water, and ice. Blend on high
speed for several minutes until smooth.

**GLUTEN-FREE // VEGAN**

# SMOOTHIE BOWLS
## *FOR A NOURISHING JUMP-START*

### RAD RASPBERRY BEET SMOOTHIE BOWL

1 heaping cup frozen raspberries

1 medium beet, cooked and peeled*

1 cup plain, whole milk yogurt

1 tablespoon virgin coconut oil or almond butter

3 or 4 dates, pitted

½ cup rolled oats

Topping ideas: sliced kiwi, fresh berries, chia seeds, pumpkin seeds, coconut flakes, cacao nibs, honey

*See page 52 for instructions on quick-cooking beets.*

### TROPICAL GREEN SMOOTHIE BOWL

1 heaping cup frozen mango or pineapple

1 frozen banana

1 cup baby spinach or chopped kale

½ ripe avocado

¾ cup unsweetened almond milk or coconut milk

Juice of 1 lime

3 or 4 dates, pitted

½ cup rolled oats (gluten-free if sensitive)

Topping ideas: sliced banana, fresh mango, dates, pecans, walnuts, chia seeds, coconut flakes, honey

Start your day right with these mouthwatering, eye-candy smoothie bowls that sneak in both a serving of fruit and veggies. The addition of healthy fats helps your body absorb all the goodness in these bowls since fat is essential for nutrient absorption.

Don't skimp on the toppings. Have fun decorating your bowl with your favorite mix-ins to guarantee a happy, not hangry, start to your day. **SERVES 2**

Blend all the ingredients except the oats and toppings on high speed until smooth. Stir in the oats and let sit for 15 minutes. Divide between 2 bowls and sprinkle on your favorite toppings. If you're cooking for 1, cover and refrigerate the extra bowl for the next day.

**GLUTEN-FREE:** Use certified gluten-free oats. // **VEGAN:** Tropical Green Smoothie Bowl // **VEGETARIAN:** Rad Raspberry Beet Smoothie Bowl

 This was Shalane's favorite recovery meal after hard workouts while training at high altitude in Mammoth. Smoothie bowls are hydrating and provide the ideal balance of fat, protein, and carbs.

Blend the ingredients and stir in the oats before you hit the sack. Cover and refrigerate. Add the toppings in the morning.

# PEACHY GREEN SMOOTHIE

## FOR A REFRESHING START TO YOUR DAY

1 heaping cup sliced peaches (fresh or frozen)*

1 frozen banana

2 cups spinach or kale

1½ cups coconut water or water

½ cup whole milk yogurt

10 to 12 fresh mint leaves

2 tablespoons almond butter

3 dates, pitted (optional)**

*If you don't have peaches, sub in frozen mango, pineapple, or blueberries.

**When we make this with water, we add the dates for a hint of sweetness. If you're using coconut water, there's no need to add the dates. A high-speed blender is recommended, if using the dates.

For rushed mornings, this smoothie can be made the night before. Simply stir in the a.m. and slurp while you do 15 minutes of Shalane's Active Recovery Stretches (page 168).

This refreshing veggie and fruit smoothie was inspired by Shalane's childhood summer days spent in Boulder, Colorado. Mint grew wild in her backyard, and she loved to pick it for drinks and salads.

The combo of probiotic-rich yogurt, enzyme-rich fruit, and revitalizing mint makes this the ideal smoothie for enhancing digestion. From experiencing the long porta-potty lines on race day, we know most runners need more gut-soothing foods.

**SERVES 2**

In a blender, combine the peaches, banana, spinach or kale, coconut water or water, yogurt, mint, almond butter, and dates, if using. Blend on high speed for several minutes until smooth.

**GLUTEN-FREE // VEGETARIAN**

*Shalane running with teammate Emily Infeld at high-altitude training camp in St. Moritz, Switzerland.*

# RACE DAY OATMEAL II: CAN'T BEET CHOCOLATE

**FOR LASTING STAMINA**

½ cup instant oats

2 or 3 dates, chopped

2 tablespoons chopped roasted almonds

1 tablespoon chia seeds

1 tablespoon chocolate chips

1 teaspoon unsweetened cocoa powder

1 teaspoon beet powder (optional)*

Pinch of sea salt

Unsweetened almond milk, to taste

*Organic, raw beet powder can be found at health food grocery stores or online.*

Make several individual-serving size batches at once and store in zipper sandwich bags.

In between writing cookbooks and nutrition coaching, Elyse can be found in her kitchen developing new recipes and products for Picky Bars, a bad-ass real-food energy bar company started by three elite athletes based in Bend, Oregon. Lucky for us, Picky Bars agreed to share one of their favorite performance oatmeal recipes developed by Elyse.

Most store-bought instant oatmeal packets are lacking in sustenance and loaded with sugar, so ditch those for our balanced oatmeal that provides easy-to-digest quick fuel and long-lasting energy. Tote premixed bags along to your next race to whip up in your hotel room or look for Picky Oats online and in select natural grocery, specialty running, bike, and outdoor stores. **SERVES 1**

**1**  In a cereal bowl, combine the oats, dates, almonds, chia seeds, chocolate chips, cocoa powder, beet powder (if using), and salt. Add 1 cup of boiling water, stir, and cover.

**2**  Allow oats to steep for 3 minutes. Stir in milk to desired consistency. Top with fresh fruit like sliced banana or berries.

**VEGAN // GLUTEN-FREE:** Use certified gluten-free oats.

# SUPERHERO MUFFINS x 3

*FOR MUFFINS THAT SUSTAIN*

2 cups almond meal*

1½ cups old-fashioned rolled oats

2 teaspoons ground cinnamon

1 teaspoon baking soda

½ teaspoon fine sea salt

½ cup walnuts, raisins, or chocolate chips (optional)

3 eggs

1 cup grated Granny Smith apple (about 1 apple)

1 cup grated carrots (about 2 carrots), peeled

6 tablespoons unsalted butter, melted

½ cup honey

*If you have a high-powered blender, you can make your own almond meal (flour). For 2 cups of almond meal, pulse 10 ounces of whole raw almonds on high speed until finely ground.*

### Nut Allergy?

We love the buttery richness of the almond flour, but whole-wheat pastry flour or whole-wheat flour can be used as an alternative in any of the Superhero Muffins. Increase the butter to 8 tablespoons (1 stick), since wheat flour is much drier, and reduce the oats to 1 cup.

Superhero Muffins are back by popular demand. This time we're giving you three incredible new flavor combos. All versions still contain hidden veggies—shh, don't tell!

As requested (we heard ya!), we came up with enough substitutions to make us go crazy in our test kitchen. We've tweaked every recipe to ensure it turns out equally delicious whether you're making it gluten-free, nut-free, or dairy-free/vegan (see variation options that follow). So go crazy and get baking!

**MAKES 12**

## APPLE CARROT

We had every muffin kid-tested, and this flavor was the clear winner among the young'uns. Shalane likes to sweeten them up by adding chocolate chips.

---

**1** Position a rack in the center of the oven. Preheat the oven to 350°F. Line a 12-cup standard muffin tin with paper muffin cups.

**2** In a large bowl, combine the almond meal, oats, cinnamon, baking soda, salt, and walnuts, raisins, or chocolate chips (if using).

**3** In a separate bowl, whisk together the eggs, apple, carrot, melted butter, and honey. Add to the dry ingredients, mixing until just combined.

**4** Spoon the batter into the muffin cups, filling each to the brim. Bake until the muffins are nicely browned on top and a knife inserted in the center of a muffin comes out clean, 25 to 30 minutes. Allow muffins to cool completely before storing.

**5** Store leftover muffins in an airtight container in the fridge or freezer. If you like them warm, reheat on low power in the microwave.

**GLUTEN-FREE:** Use certified gluten-free oats.

# SUPERHERO MUFFINS x 3

2 cups almond meal
(see note, page 60)

1½ cups old-fashioned
rolled oats

1 tablespoon pumpkin pie
spice

1 teaspoon baking soda

½ teaspoon fine sea salt

½ cup walnuts, raisins, or
chocolate chips (optional)

3 eggs

1½ cups canned pumpkin
puree (unsweetened)*

6 tablespoons unsalted
butter, melted

½ cup maple syrup

*Use up leftover pumpkin
puree by tossing it into a
smoothie.*

## PUMPKIN SPICE

Make this flavor for snacks to get you through a dreary winter week or bake up a batch for friends at a holiday brunch.

**1** Position a rack in the center of the oven. Preheat the oven to 350°F. Line a 12-cup standard muffin tin with paper muffin cups.

**2** In a large bowl, combine the almond meal, oats, pumpkin pie spice, baking soda, salt, and walnuts, raisins, or chocolate chips (if using).

**3** In a separate bowl, whisk together the eggs, pumpkin puree, melted butter, and syrup. Add to the dry ingredients, mixing until just combined.

**4** Spoon the batter into the muffin cups, filling each to the brim. Bake until the muffins are nicely browned on top and a knife inserted in the center of a muffin comes out clean, 30 to 35 minutes.

**5** Store leftover muffins in an airtight container in the fridge or freezer. If you like them warm, reheat on low power in the microwave.

**GLUTEN-FREE:** Use certified gluten-free oats.

*"Did you give me this one [to test] because you know I'm one of the only people on the planet who eats pumpkin spice on everything all year round??? You know it's a good sign when you can't stop sneaking spoonfuls of the batter before it goes into the oven! Love it!"*

**—MATT LLANO,** *ELITE MARATHONER AND RECIPE TESTER*

# SUPERHERO MUFFINS x 3

2 cups almond meal
(see note, page 60)

1½ cups old-fashioned
rolled oats

2 teaspoons ground
cinnamon

1 teaspoon baking soda

½ teaspoon fine sea salt

1 cup grated, raw beet,
peeled (about 1 beet)

3 eggs

⅓ cup blackstrap molasses

6 tablespoons unsalted
butter, melted

1 cup frozen blueberries

Elyse likes to make
mini muffins for the
mini superheroes in her life.
If using a mini-muffin pan,
reduce the bake time by
10 minutes.

## BEET BLUEBERRY MOLASSES

This is Shalane's favorite variation while training at high-altitude, because molasses is high in blood-building iron and beets are high in natural nitrates, which may improve blood pressure. This is the least sweet of the pack. If you prefer a sweeter muffin, you can sub in a ½ cup honey for the molasses.

**1** Position a rack in the center of the oven. Preheat the oven to 350°F. Line a 12-cup standard muffin tin with paper muffin cups.

**2** In a large bowl, combine the almond meal, oats, cinnamon, baking soda, and salt.

**3** In a separate bowl, whisk together the beets, eggs, molasses, and melted butter. Add to the dry ingredients, mixing until combined. Fold in the blueberries.

**4** Spoon the batter into the muffin cups, filling each to the brim. Bake until the muffins are browned on top and a knife inserted in the center of a muffin comes out clean, 25 to 30 minutes.

**5** Store leftover muffins in an airtight container in the fridge or freezer. If you like them warm, reheat on low power in the microwave.

**GLUTEN-FREE:** Use certified gluten-free oats. // **VEGAN:** Any of these muffins can be made without eggs and butter. Sub 3 tablespoons ground flax combined with ½ cup water for the eggs (let sit for 5 minutes). And sub ¼ cup melted coconut oil for the butter.

# HONEY CARDAMOM GRANOLA

**FOR BREAKING FREE FROM BOXED CEREAL**

3 cups old-fashioned rolled oats

½ cup chopped nuts (walnuts, pecans, almonds, cashews, hazelnuts, or combo)

½ cup unsweetened coconut flakes

1 teaspoon ground cinnamon

½ teaspoon ground cardamom (can sub ground ginger)

½ teaspoon sea salt

⅓ cup honey

⅓ cup extra-virgin olive oil

1 teaspoon vanilla

Double this recipe if you devour granola as fast as we do. It stores well in a glass container in the pantry or can be stashed in a zipper bag in the freezer.

**Get Fancy:** Stir in ½ cup freeze-dried strawberries or raspberries after the granola cools.

We received so much love for our Ginger Molasses Granola on social media that we knew you'd be thrilled to have another awesome granola recipe in your lineup. This time we spiked it with cardamom for a spicy-sweet boost to start (or end) your day right. This lightly sweetened, satisfyingly salty, extra crunchy granola will help you break free from a sugary cereal addiction.

Sprinkle generously on top of whole milk yogurt for a mineral-rich, sleep-inducing late night snack (see more sleep tips on page 150). Nut-free? Leave out the nuts and sub in pumpkin or sunflower seeds. **MAKES 5 CUPS**

**1** Preheat the oven to 275°F and line a rimmed baking sheet with parchment paper.

**2** In a large mixing bowl, combine the oats, nuts, coconut, cinnamon, cardamom, and salt.

**3** Add the honey, oil, and vanilla and stir until evenly combined.

**4** Spread out on the baking sheet. Bake for 40 minutes, stirring after 20 minutes, until lightly browned. Cool completely before breaking up the clusters.

**5** Transfer to a widemouthed glass jar with a lid. Granola will stay fresh for several weeks and is likely to be devoured long before expiring.

**VEGETARIAN // GLUTEN-FREE:** Use certified gluten-free oats.

# POWER MUESLI

## FOR A.M. FUEL AT THE READY

4 cups old-fashioned rolled oats

1 cup walnuts, almonds, pecans, or cashews, chopped

½ cup dried fruit (date pieces, chopped apricots, goji berries, raisins, etc.)

⅓ cup pumpkin seeds or sunflower seeds

⅓ cup coconut flakes

¼ cup sesame seeds or ground flax

1 tablespoon ground cinnamon

On Elyse's kitchen counter, you'll always find a large glass canister filled with rolled oats and a random assortment of nuts, seeds, and dried fruit. She calls it Power Muesli and uses it to make quick weekday breakfast bowls—either by stirring it into yogurt or by simmering it with water and milk to make oatmeal.

Follow our recipe below for a muesli loaded with protein, healthy fats, antioxidants, and minerals. Or create your own concoction to use up any odd assortment of leftover baking ingredients. This is a great recipe to let your creativity shine!

**MAKES 5 CUPS**

---

Place all the above ingredients in a large glass canister or a gallon-size zipper bag and shake to combine. Use it to whip up any of the quick, hot or cold, breakfast options below.

### OVERNIGHT OATS (COLD)
In a cereal bowl, combine ½ cup muesli, ½ cup whole milk yogurt, and ⅓ cup unsweetened almond milk. Cover and leave in the fridge overnight. Just before serving, top with fresh fruit and honey. **SERVES 1**

### YOGURT BOWL (COLD)
In a cereal bowl, combine ¼ to ½ cup of muesli with ½ to 1 cup plain, whole milk yogurt. Set aside for 15 minutes to allow oats to soften. Top with chopped apple, peaches, or berries and honey. **SERVES 1**

### HOT OATMEAL
In a medium pot, bring to a boil 2½ cups of liquid (we like to use a combo of water and unsweetened almond milk). Add 1½ cups of muesli and a pinch of salt. Reduce heat to low, cover, and simmer, stirring occasionally until the oatmeal thickens, about 10 minutes. Divide between bowls, add more milk to taste, drizzle with honey or molasses, and top with fresh berries. **SERVES 2**

**GLUTEN-FREE:** Use certified gluten-free oats. // **VEGAN:** Sub coconut milk yogurt for the whole milk yogurt.

# COCONUT BANANA BREAKFAST COOKIES

**FOR BREAKFAST ON THE GO**

1½ cups old-fashioned rolled oats

1 cup shredded coconut

⅔ cup coconut flour*

½ cup walnuts or raisins

2 teaspoons ground cinnamon

½ teaspoon salt

4 eggs

½ cup mashed banana (about 1½ very ripe, brown-speckled bananas)

½ cup virgin coconut oil, melted

¼ cup honey

Coconut oil has come under scrutiny for not being as healthy as touted. Yes, it's high in saturated fat, but saturated fat can be a healthy part of a whole foods diet in moderation. When an ingredient gains celebrity status, it gets added to every type of packaged food. These foods are often high in sugar and other processed ingredients. Our best advice is to avoid these health-proclaiming packaged goods and instead bake your own treats that you can feel good about enjoying.

*Coconut flour can be found at natural food stores or online at bobsredmill.com.*

We received countless requests for nut-free, wholesome treats, since many schools don't allow snacks with nuts. Busy students and parents alike will love this allergy-friendly grab-n-go breakfast cookie.

These cookies are gluten-free, dairy-free, and nut-free, plus they're high in protein and healthy fat to set you on track for a productive day. They're slightly sweetened with honey and bananas, making them low on the glycemic index, which is ideal for balanced energy. **MAKES 24 SMALL COOKIES**

**1** Preheat the oven to 350°F and line two baking sheets with parchment paper.

**2** In a large bowl, combine the oats, coconut, coconut flour, walnuts or raisins, cinnamon, and salt. Add the eggs, banana, coconut oil, and honey and stir thoroughly.

**3** Roll dough into golf ball–size balls, space 2 inches apart on the baking sheets, and flatten slightly. Bake for 16 to 20 minutes, or until the bottoms are golden brown.

**VEGETARIAN** // **GLUTEN-FREE:** Use certified gluten-free oats.

# PEACHES AND MOLASSES QUINOA BOWL

*FOR NOURISHING YOUR INNER WARRIOR*

¾ cup cooked quinoa
(see cooking instructions,
page 90)

½ cup unsweetened
almond milk or other milk
of choice

¼ cup favorite mix-ins*

½ ripe peach, chopped

Blackstrap molasses
(or honey), to taste

Sprinkle of cinnamon

*Use any combo of nuts,
seeds, dried fruit, chia seeds,
coconut flakes, or ground flax.*

Just 1 tablespoon of
blackstrap molasses
contains 20 percent of your
daily value of iron. Bam!

With the protein-packed, mineral-rich power combo of quinoa, nuts, and seeds, we imagine this would be the modern-day breakfast of choice for Inca warriors. Unleash your own warrior within by enlisting this satisfying bowl as your weekday breakfast.

The next time you're making quinoa for a salad, double the batch so you have enough leftover to make this breakfast in 5 minutes tops. **SERVES 1**

In a microwave-safe cereal bowl, combine the quinoa, milk, and mix-ins. Microwave until warm. Top with the peaches, drizzle with molasses (or honey), and sprinkle with cinnamon.

**GLUTEN-FREE** // **VEGAN**

# SHALANE'S STRENGTH ROUTINE

To improve performance, increase strength, and help prevent injuries, Shalane gets into the weight room 3 times per week. Here are her favorite exercises that you can do in your own home. Repeat each exercise 2 or 3 times.

---

## >> AB RIPPER

Lie flat on your back with your arms at your side and palms facing down. Bring your legs off the ground and knees to your chest, then pike your legs straight up into the air while engaging your core and trying to keep a neutral spine. Bring your legs back down. Repeat 10 to 20 times.

## >> GLUTE DUCK WALK

Place a resistance band around your ankles and slightly bend at your knees. Walk forward 20 steps with your legs at least hip-width apart and then return to your starting point by walking backward. Keep your butt activated and your weight distributed across your whole foot, not just your forefoot. You should feel resistance on the side of your legs, and your glutes should burn.

## >> OBLIQUE CRUNCH

Lie on your side on an exercise ball with your feet slightly spread apart and pressed up against a wall. Bend the upper half of your body over the ball and then crunch up toward your feet. You should feel your obliques engage. Go slowly and don't let the ball bounce you up. Do 20 crunches on each side.

## >> RUNNING SHOES ARM LIFTS

Hold a running shoe in each hand at your sides with your palms facing down. Stand tall, keep your arms straight, and lift straight out from quad to shoulder height. Repeat 10 times. Next, lift your arms out to a V-angle 10 times. Finally, lift your arms straight out from your sides 10 times.

## >> SQUAT TO HIGH KNEE

Place your feet shoulder-width apart with your toes facing forward, your butt back, and your weight in the heels of your feet. Squat down and, as you come up, raise one leg into a high-knee running position, stand tall, and hold this position for 2 seconds. Alternate bringing up your right and left leg for 20 counts.

## >> HAMSTRING CURLS ON BALL

Lie on the floor on your back and place your heels on top of the middle of an exercise ball. Activate your core and glutes and raise your butt off the floor while pressing your heels into the ball. Hold this position for 10 counts, then lift up and down for 10, then hold for 10 counts. Last, curl the ball toward your butt with your heels while keeping your butt and hips even and raised.

"Overprepare and then go with the flow."

—SHALANE

# 4 | LONG RUN BRUNCH

*"There's not a better feeling than when you
have found that moment of balance and
harmony when both running and life come
together. Then you know why you run and
that you couldn't live without it."*

**–JOAN BENOIT SAMUELSON**

# TEMPEH SCRAMBLE
## FOR A PROTEIN-PACKED START

1 (8-ounce) package tempeh

2 tablespoons white or mellow miso

2 tablespoons extra-virgin olive oil

1 yellow onion, sliced

¼ teaspoon fine sea salt

4 cups chopped kale, stems removed

1 teaspoon dried oregano

½ teaspoon fennel seeds (optional)

¼ teaspoon red pepper flakes (optional)

1 avocado, sliced (optional)

Meat and vegetable lovers alike will gain a newfound appreciation for tempeh once they try this protein-packed scramble that's worthy of breakfast or dinner. Tempeh is made from whole, fermented soybeans, making it high on the nutrient scale: probiotics, B vitamins, calcium, iron, and more!

Tempeh requires time to marinate to get rid of its natural bitterness, so prep this recipe before you head out for your run. Transform the leftovers into dinner by serving taco-style in warm tortillas or on top of rice with homemade guacamole (see page 177) and/or salsa (see page 176). **SERVES 3**

**1** Use your hands to crumble the tempeh into small pieces. In a medium bowl, whisk the miso into ½ cup of water until dissolved. Add the tempeh and marinate for at least 1 hour or overnight in the fridge.

**2** Heat the oil in a large sauté pan over medium heat. Add the onion and salt and cook for 5 minutes, stirring occasionally, until the onion begins to caramelize.

**3** Add the tempeh, miso marinade, kale, oregano, fennel seeds (if using), and red pepper flakes (if using) to the pan and cook, stirring occasionally, for an additional 5 minutes. Serve topped with sliced avocado.

**GLUTEN-FREE // VEGAN**

# STEADFAST EGG SCRAMBLE
## *FOR EGG-CELLENT RECOVERY*

4 or 5 eggs

⅓ cup crumbled feta
(or other cheese)

½ teaspoon dried oregano

1 tablespoon extra-virgin
olive oil

1 cup leftover Sunday
Sweet Potatoes (page 161)
or other roasted veggie

1 small avocado, sliced

Coarse sea salt and ground
pepper, to taste

---

The labeling on eggs at the grocery store is highly confusing and misleading. "Cage free" does not mean the chicken is actually enjoying a free life, plucking grasses and bugs out on the open range. The chicken may still be confined to a barn and fed an unnatural diet of corn and soy. The best bet is to buy your eggs direct from a local farmer you trust. Once you taste and see an egg from a truly free-range chicken, you'll never go back.

This is our go-to egg scramble that you'll find us devouring for recovery after morning runs. It takes the same amount of time as your average scrambled eggs, but provides the ultimate combo of easy-to-digest complete protein, complex carbs, and healthy fats.

Elyse loves to whip up this scramble after long weekend trail runs on the Deschutes River. Shalane likes to make this dish post tempo workouts for egg-cellent recovery. **SERVES 2**

---

**1** In a small bowl, whisk together the eggs, feta, and oregano.

**2** Heat the oil in a nonstick pan over medium heat. Sauté the sweet potatoes just until warm. Add the egg mixture and cook, using a flexible spatula to stir and scrape from the bottom, until the eggs are set, about 2 minutes.

**3** Top with the avocado. Add salt and pepper to taste.

**GLUTEN-FREE // VEGETARIAN // DAIRY-FREE:** Skip the cheese.

# APPLE PIE STEEL-CUT OATMEAL

*FOR A WHOLESOME START*

### OATMEAL

1 cup steel-cut oats

2 cups water

1 cup milk of choice

¼ teaspoon fine sea salt

### SAUTÉED APPLES

2 tablespoons virgin coconut oil or butter

2 large Granny Smith apples, chopped bite-size

½ cup chopped pecans

¼ cup maple syrup

2 teaspoons ground cinnamon

---

This recipe was a breakfast favorite for Shalane during her intense training for the NYC Marathon.

The night before, bring 2 cups of water to a boil, stir in the oats, turn off the heat, cover, and leave out overnight. In the morning, add the milk and salt and simmer for 10 minutes while you cook the apples.

Runners love their oatmeal, but bland oats can get pretty tiresome day in and day out. This recipe for slow-simmered steel-cut oats topped with caramelized apples takes oatmeal to a whole new level of awesomeness. Sure it takes more time to cook, but these energizing oats are guaranteed to take you places (check out our time-saving tip below).

Oats are an easy-to-digest complex carb for lasting energy. They're high in the soluble fiber beta-glucan, an immune system booster. Oats and an apple a day keep the doc away! **SERVES 4**

---

**1** To make the oatmeal: In a large saucepan bring the oats, water, milk, and salt to a boil. Turn heat to low, cover and simmer for 30 minutes, stirring every 10 minutes, until the oats are soft and chewy.

**2** To make the apples: Heat the oil or butter in a skillet over medium-high heat, add the apples, and sauté, stirring occasionally, until they begin to brown, about 10 minutes. Remove from the heat. Stir in the pecans, maple syrup, and cinnamon.

**3** Stir half of the caramelized apple-pecan mixture into the oatmeal. Divide oatmeal between cereal bowls and top with the remaining apple-pecan mixture. Serve hot.

**4** Leftovers can be reheated in the microwave. Simply add more milk until desired consistency is reached.

**GLUTEN-FREE:** Use certified gluten-free oats. **// VEGAN:** Use nut milk.

# SPINACH AND SAUSAGE FRITTATA

**FOR PRONTO PROTEIN**

9 eggs

¼ cup plain whole milk yogurt

1 teaspoon dried oregano

¼ teaspoon fine sea salt

1 tablespoon extra-virgin olive oil

2 mild Italian sausages (chicken or pork), chopped

½ yellow onion, chopped

4 cups baby spinach

½ cup grated Parmesan

While you wait for the frittata to bake, try Shalane's Active Recovery Stretches (page 168).

Frittatas are our saving grace on busy weeknights when we need a protein-packed meal pronto. This dish is the ultimate in adaptability as it can be served any time of day—chow down for a hearty brunch, pack a wedge in a glass container for lunch to go, or serve alongside a salad for a complete dinner.

Get creative—frittatas are a great way to use up any assortment of leftover veggies. **SERVES 6**

**1** Preheat the oven to 375°F. In a large bowl, whisk together the eggs, yogurt, oregano, and salt. Set aside.

**2** Heat the oil in a 10-inch to 12-inch oven-safe skillet over medium-high heat. Add the sausage and onion and cook, stirring occasionally, until they begin to brown, about 5 minutes. Add the spinach and cook just until wilted. Remove skillet from heat.

**3** Pour the egg mixture over top and lightly stir to evenly spread out the spinach and sausage. Sprinkle the Parmesan on top.

**4** Bake in the center of the oven for 25 minutes, or until the eggs have set and the top is golden. Cut into 6 slices and serve.

**GLUTEN-FREE // VEGETARIAN:** Sub in leftover roasted potatoes (see Sunday Sweet Potatoes, page 161, or Roasted Cauliflower and Potatoes, page 162) for the sausage.

# OATMEAL BANANA PANCAKES

## FOR THE ULTIMATE RUNNER'S STACK

1⅓ cups oat flour*

½ cup all-purpose flour

2 teaspoons baking powder

½ teaspoon fine sea salt

1 cup milk of choice

¾ cup mashed, ripe banana (about 2 bananas)

2 eggs

2 tablespoons butter or virgin coconut oil, melted, plus more for frying

1 teaspoon vanilla

½ cup frozen blueberries (optional)

Topping ideas: butter, maple syrup, peanut butter, and/or sliced banana

*Make your own oat flour by pulsing 1½ cups rolled oats in a high-speed blender until it's the consistency of coarse flour. Oat flour can also be found at most grocery stores or you can sub in whole-wheat flour.

If you dream of pancakes while you're out on your long run, you are not alone. It's a totally normal attribute of us dedicated runners to fantasize about our next meal while pounding the pavement. Cure your stack craving with these guilt-free, sugar-free, oatmeal pancakes. Prep the batter (while you wait for that cup of coffee to work its magic!) before you head out the door. This recipe makes a large enough stack to share with your running partner. **MAKES 15 3-INCH PANCAKES**

---

**1**  In a large mixing bowl, combine the flours, baking powder, and salt.

**2**  In a separate bowl, whisk together the milk, banana, eggs, melted butter or coconut oil, and vanilla.

**3**  Add the wet ingredients to the dry and stir just until combined. Stir in the blueberries (if using). Let the batter rest for 15 minutes (or until you get back from your run).

**4**  Heat a large cast-iron pan or griddle over medium heat. Add about a tablespoon of the butter or coconut oil to the pan and swirl to coat. Spoon the batter into the pan. Cook until bubbles begin to form in the center of the pancakes, about 3 minutes. Flip the cakes and cook until well browned, about 3 minutes.

**5**  Top with more butter and maple syrup or smother with peanut butter and sliced banana.

**6**  Store leftover batter covered in the fridge for up to 3 days or store leftover cooked pancakes in a zipper bag in the freezer between layers of parchment paper. Pop in the toaster to reheat.

### IRON CAKES

Take these pancakes to the next level by blending the milk with 2 heaping cups of spinach prior to adding it to the batter. Now you've got green pancakes. We call them Iron Cakes!

**VEGETARIAN  //  DAIRY-FREE:** Use nut milk.

# WILD RICE PANCAKES
## FOR PANCAKES ANYTIME OF DAY

1 cup almond meal

½ teaspoon baking soda

½ teaspoon fine sea salt

1½ cups cooked wild rice, well drained and cooled*

3 scallions, white and green parts, chopped

½ cup unsweetened almond milk or whole milk

2 eggs

¼ cup virgin coconut oil, divided

*To cook wild rice: Bring 4 cups water and ½ teaspoon of salt to a boil in a large saucepan. Add 1 cup wild rice, reduce the heat, cover, and simmer until the rice grains burst open and are soft but chewy, 35 to 40 minutes. Drain the rice and transfer to a large bowl to cool. A cup of uncooked wild rice makes about 3 cups of cooked rice. Use leftover rice in Power Bowls (page 122).

Meal prep on Sundays to save time midweek. The rice can be cooked up to 4 days in advance.

Gluten-free pancake mixes are high in refined grains and additives. These cakes are made with whole wild rice for a wholesome start (or end) to your day. Wild rice is a great source of protein and essential minerals for bone health. Since it's a grass, not a grain, it's also easy to digest.

You can serve these pancakes sweet-style with a drizzle of maple syrup or savory-style by topping them with a fried egg. Leftovers are definitely worthy of dinner, especially when you top 'em with a smear of cream cheese and decadent smoked salmon.

**MAKES 10 3-INCH PANCAKES**

---

**1** In a large bowl, combine almond meal, baking soda, and salt. Add the rice, scallions, milk, eggs, and 2 tablespoons of melted coconut oil and stir until well combined. If the batter is too thick to spread out in the pan, add another splash of milk (this will likely be needed if your rice sat overnight in the fridge).

**2** Heat a cast-iron skillet or frying pan over medium heat. Add about a tablespoon of the remaining oil and swirl to coat the pan. Spoon the batter into the pan to form 3-inch pancakes. Fry for 3 to 4 minutes or until golden brown. Flip the cakes and cook on the opposite side for 2 to 3 minutes.

**3** Continue with the remaining batter, adding more oil between batches. If leftover batter sticks to the pan, carefully wipe clean with a folded paper towel before adding more oil.

**4** Serve immediately or allow pancakes to cool and store leftovers in an airtight container in the fridge or freeze. Reheat pancakes by popping in the toaster.

**GLUTEN-FREE // VEGETARIAN // NUT-FREE:** Sub in 1 cup whole-wheat flour for the almond meal.

# SWEET POTATO WAFFLES (OR PANCAKES)

*FOR CARBS WORTH LOADING*

2 cups whole-wheat pastry flour*

2 tablespoons coconut sugar (or white sugar)

2 teaspoons baking powder

2 teaspoons ground cinnamon

½ teaspoon fine sea salt

3 eggs

1¼ cups whole milk or unsweetened almond milk

1 cup mashed orange-fleshed sweet potatoes (yams)**

4 tablespoons butter, melted

*Don't have pastry flour? Sub in 1 cup whole-wheat flour and 1 cup all-purpose flour.*

**Outta sweet potatoes? Sub in mashed banana or pumpkin puree. Batter will be slightly thicker, so add a little extra milk to thin.*

Sneak veggies into breakfast! This versatile batter makes unbeatable Belgian-style waffles or fluffy pancakes. Add a side of scrambled eggs and you've got yourself the ideal recovery brunch for celebrating after a long Sunday run.

Cook 'em in advance so breakfast is waiting for you when you walk in the door feeling famished. Simply reheat in the toaster and they'll pop up warm and crispy. Drizzle with maple syrup for added bliss. **SERVES 6**

---

**1**  In a large bowl, combine the flour, sugar, baking powder, cinnamon, and salt.

**2**  In a separate bowl, whisk together the eggs, milk, sweet potatoes, and butter.

**3**  Add the wet ingredients to the dry and mix just until combined.

**4**  To make waffles: Heat a waffle iron and brush with a high-heat oil. Ladle the batter into each waffle slot, being careful not to overfill. Cook until golden brown. Set the waffles aside and continue with the remaining batter.

**5**  To make pancakes: Add a little extra milk to thin the batter. Heat a large cast-iron pan or griddle over medium-low heat. Add a small amount of high-heat oil to the pan and swirl to coat. Spoon the batter into the pan. Cook until bubbles begin to form in the center of the pancakes. Flip the cakes and cook until browned.

**6**  Store leftovers in the fridge for up to 1 week or the freezer for up to 3 months. Reheat in the toaster.

**VEGETARIAN // DAIRY-FREE:** Use nut milk and sub coconut oil for the butter.

# AVOCADO TOAST WITH GREENS
## FOR A FAT START TO THE DAY

2 slices whole-grain bread

1 ripe avocado, halved

½ cup leftover sautéed greens (see Miso Fast Greens, page 167)

2 fried eggs (see "Two Perfect Fried Eggs," below)

---

Need an immunity boost? After toasting the bread, rub it with a clove of peeled garlic. Raw garlic has both antiviral and antibacterial properties to help fend off cold viruses.

If you haven't hopped on the avocado toast bandwagon, you're seriously missing out. Avocados are high in monounsaturated fats, fiber, vitamin K, vitamin C, vitamin B6, folate, and potassium. Starting your day with healthy fats helps jump-start your metabolism and will keep you satiated until lunch.

We love to dress up our avocado toast with a heaping of greens (say yes to veggies for breakfast!) and a fried egg with an oozy, enticing yolk. Add a second egg if you're in training mode.

**SERVES 2**

---

1  Toast the bread. Scoop half an avocado onto each slice and smash with the back of a fork.

2  Divide the greens on top of the avocado, top with a fried egg, and add salt and pepper to taste.

3  This toast is best eaten with a fork and knife.

**VEGETARIAN // GLUTEN-FREE:** Use gluten-free bread.

---

## TWO PERFECT FRIED EGGS

A flawless fried egg transforms simple dishes like rice bowls, grain salads, and avocado toast. The goal is crispy edges with the whites fully cooked and the yolks still runny. You want that yolk to ooze like a luscious sauce when your fork first dives into the center. Fried eggs cook fast, so have the rest of your meal ready before you begin.

Heat a nonstick pan or skillet over medium-high heat. Add enough oil to coat the bottom of the pan. Crack an egg onto each side of the pan. Sprinkle with salt and pepper. Cook just until the white sets, about 1 minute and 30 seconds. Carefully flip the egg and cook on the second side for 30 seconds.

# APPLE CHEDDAR SCONES

*FOR BRUNCH WITH FRIENDS*

1⅓ cups whole-wheat flour

1⅓ cups whole-wheat pastry flour or all-purpose flour

1 tablespoon baking powder

½ teaspoon baking soda

1 teaspoon fine sea salt (reduce if butter is salted)

1 stick (8 tablespoons) unsalted butter

2 cups chopped Granny Smith apple (about 1 large)

1 cup grated cheddar cheese, divided

2 tablespoons chopped fresh rosemary or 2 teaspoons dried rosemary (optional)

1⅓ cups plain, whole milk yogurt (not Greek-style)

If you're ever in Portland, it's worth making a trip to Tabor Bread to experience bread bliss with zero guilt. At Tabor they grind on site organic, whole grains into wholesome flour. This recipe is inspired by the whole-grain, don't-skimp-on-the-butter scones from this awesome institution.

We love baking with whole-wheat flour because it has a nuttier flavor and a heartier texture. It's also less refined than white flour and is higher in fiber and nutrients. **MAKES 12**

**1** Preheat the oven to 350°F. Line a standard baking sheet with parchment paper.

**2** In a large bowl, mix together the flours, baking powder, baking soda, and salt.

**3** Cut the butter into 1-inch cubes and add to the bowl. Using a pastry cutter or your fingers, break up the butter into pieces and incorporate into the flour. If using your hands, work quickly to keep the butter cold.

**4** Mix in the apple, ½ cup of the cheese, and rosemary (if using). Add the yogurt and mix until the dough begins to come together and then use your hands to incorporate any remaining flour.

**5** Place the dough onto a lightly floured surface and shape into a 1½-inch-thick flattened log about 20 inches long. Cut the log into 12 triangles and place on the baking sheet. Press remaining cheese on top of each scone.

**6** Bake for 25 to 30 minutes, or until golden brown.

**7** Leftover scones can be stored in the fridge or freezer. Thaw and reheat in the oven at 300°F for 10 to 15 minutes, or until warm and flaky.

**VEGETARIAN**

# 5 | LUNCH PAIL
## (& SALADS)

*"Seek a calling. Even if you don't know what that means, seek it. If you're following your calling, the fatigue will be easier to bear, the disappointments will be fuel, the highs will be like nothing you've ever felt."*

**–PHIL KNIGHT,** SHOE DOG

# THAI QUINOA SALAD

## FOR FIGHTING INFLAMMATION

1 cup quinoa, rinsed and drained

2 cups grated carrots (about 2 large)

2 cups thinly sliced purple cabbage

3 green onions, white and green parts sliced

1 cup packed mint leaves, chopped (cilantro works too)

1 cup packed basil leaves, chopped

1 jalapeño or serrano pepper, seeds removed, minced (optional)

½ cup roasted peanuts, chopped

### DRESSING

¼ cup extra-virgin olive oil

⅓ cup fresh lime juice (2 to 3 limes)

2 tablespoons soy sauce or tamari

2 tablespoons honey (or maple syrup)

1 tablespoon fish sauce (optional)

Use a food processor to grate the carrots and chop the cabbage and herbs.

Cook a double batch of quinoa and save the leftovers for breakfast. Our Peaches and Molasses Quinoa Bowl (page 69) is a satisfying alternative to sugary cereal.

When Shalane traveled to Bend, Oregon, to kick off recipe testing for book two with Elyse, this was the very first recipe to come out of Elyse's kitchen. It was love at first bite. We continued to tweak the recipe, not because it needed much work, but because we secretly wanted an excuse to make it time and again. This is the salad Shalane made on a near weekly basis while training for the 2017 NYC Marathon and 2018 Boston Marathon.

We highly recommend the use of fish sauce (a store-bought condiment) to give the salad a true Thai-inspired umami kick, but if you're vegan or vegetarian, the salad is crown-worthy made with just soy sauce.

Make this salad on a Sunday night for work lunches all week long or serve as a side dish with a juicy, grilled steak for a dinner set to impress. **SERVES 5**

1 Here is a foolproof method to cook quinoa: In a medium saucepan over high heat, bring to a boil 1½ cups water and the quinoa. Reduce the heat to low and simmer, covered, for 15 minutes or until all the water has been absorbed. Transfer to a large salad bowl, fluff with a fork, and set aside to cool.

2 Meanwhile, put the olive oil, lime juice, soy sauce or tamari, honey, and fish sauce (if using) in a glass jar or bowl and stir to combine.

3 Once the quinoa is cool, add the carrots, cabbage, onion, mint, basil, and pepper (if using) to the bowl and toss to combine. Add the dressing and toss again. Taste and, if needed, add more fish sauce or soy sauce.

4 Top with the peanuts. Chill in the fridge for at least 1 hour or until ready to serve.

5 This salad will stay fresh in airtight glass containers in the fridge for up to 5 days.

**GLUTEN-FREE // VEGAN:** Omit the fish sauce.

# TUNA WHITE BEAN SALAD

*FOR A FEED-ME-FAST MEAL*

1 can (5 ounces) tuna,
drained

1 cup cannellini beans
(or other white bean),
rinsed and drained

¼ cup finely chopped
red onion

2 tablespoons chopped
Kalamata olives (optional)

3 tablespoons balsamic
vinegar

2 tablespoons extra-virgin
olive oil

⅛ teaspoon sea salt

Ground pepper

While Elyse was working abroad in Switzerland, this salad became a dependable weeknight, no-fuss meal in her home. Elyse likes to eat this protein-packed salad on top of arugula with a hunk of baguette.

When buying canned tuna, look for brands that practice sustainable fishing practices and test their fish for harmful contaminants like mercury. Our two favorite brands are Wild Planet and Safe Catch. **SERVES 2**

---

**1**  In a medium-size bowl, combine the tuna, beans, onion, olives (if using), vinegar, oil, salt, and a few grinds of pepper. Taste and add more salt and pepper, if needed.

**2**  Serve on top of salad greens or whole-grain toast.

**GLUTEN-FREE**

*Nike Bowerman Track Club women at training camp in Park City, Utah, before the 2016 Rio Summer Olympic Games. (left to right) Colleen Quigley, Shelby Houlihan, Courtney Frerichs, Shalane Flanagan, Emily Infeld, and Amy Cragg.*

# CURRY EGG SALAD
## *FOR A HEALTHY MAKEOVER TO A CLASSIC*

**DRESSING**

¼ cup plain whole milk yogurt

1 tablespoon apple cider vinegar

2 teaspoons curry powder

1 teaspoon Dijon mustard

¼ teaspoon fine sea salt

**SALAD**

4 hard-boiled eggs, peeled*

½ cup chopped apple

½ cup chopped celery

¼ cup chopped walnuts (optional)

2 scallions, white and green parts, sliced (optional)

*\*To make perfect hard-boiled eggs, bring a large saucepan of water to a boil. Use a spoon to lower eggs into the water. Simmer for 10 minutes. Submerge eggs in ice water to stop the cooking and make them easier to peel. Store eggs unpeeled in the fridge for up to 1 week. For even more speed, use an Instant Pot.*

Egg salad reminds us of childhood lunches at grandma's house. But we promise this egg salad in no way resembles the mayo-saturated, gloppy egg salad of yesteryear. It's creamy, savory, sweet, and spicy to satisfy all your taste buds.

Shalane loves to devour it piled on thick sliced whole-grain toast after a morning workout. Elyse likes it on top of salad greens topped with Crispy Chickpeas (page 196). **SERVES 2**

---

**1**  In medium bowl, whisk together the yogurt, vinegar, curry powder, mustard, and salt. Add the eggs and smash with a fork. Stir in the apple, celery, walnuts (if using), and scallions (if using).

**2**  Serve on top of salad greens or toast or wrap in a tortilla.

**GLUTEN-FREE // VEGETARIAN**

# DIY GRAIN SALAD

*FOR A SALAD THAT SUSTAINS*

1 cup whole grains, rinsed using a fine-mesh strainer

1 bunch kale, stems removed, finely chopped

2 cups seasonal veggies, chopped or grated*

½ cup something salty (Parmesan, feta, olives)

½ cup chopped roasted nuts or seeds (almonds, walnuts, pumpkin seeds, sunflower seeds)

1 recipe Apple Cider Vinaigrette (page 186)

*\* Mix it up based on what's in season. Favorites include carrots, tomatoes, peppers, cucumbers, peas, radishes, fennel, avocado, leftover grilled zucchini or asparagus, or leftover roasted veggies (beets, cauliflower, Brussels sprouts, sweet potatoes, and butternut squash). Grain salads are also stellar tossed with our Lemon or Orange Miso Dressing (page 184).*

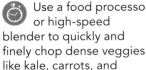 This salad also makes a killer wrap for lunch on the go. Smear a whole-wheat tortilla with goat cheese, pile on the salad, and roll it tightly closed.

Use a food processor or high-speed blender to quickly and finely chop dense veggies like kale, carrots, and raw beets.

Every Sunday Elyse throws together a hearty grain salad for quick work lunches during the week. The base of her go-to protein-packed salads is typically quinoa or farro and kale and then she dresses it up with any assortment of seasonal veggies. She always tops it off with a generous amount of homemade vinaigrette.

Have fun experimenting with a variety of whole grains as the base like farro, kamut, freekah, wild rice, or quinoa. If you're short on time, sub in a can of chickpeas (simply rinse and drain) for the grains. **SERVES 5**

---

**1** Cook your grain of choice according to the package directions, being careful not to overcook (you want your grains to have enough texture to hold up to the dressing). For quinoa, we recommend using less water than typically recommended (see our foolproof quinoa cooking method on page 90). Set aside in a large salad bowl to cool.

**2** Add the kale, veggies, cheese or olives, and nuts or seeds to the grains and toss to combine. Add the dressing and salt and pepper to taste (go generous on the dressing as the grains will sop it up).

**3** This salad gets even better the next day, so don't be afraid to make it in advance.

**VEGETARIAN** // **VEGAN:** Use olives instead of cheese. // **GLUTEN-FREE:** Use quinoa or wild rice.

# KALE AND EDAMAME ORANGE MISO SALAD

## FOR IRON-RICH NOURISHMENT

5 cups packed chopped kale (1 large bunch), stems removed

1 recipe Orange Miso Dressing (page 184)

1 cup grated carrot (about 2 carrots), peeled

1 large navel orange, peeled and chopped

1 cup shelled edamame, cooked according to package directions and cooled

½ cup roasted almonds, chopped

5 green onions (scallions), sliced (optional)

High school runner Eliza Medearis won the *Run Fast. Eat Slow.* recipe contest by submitting this refreshing and satisfying salad, which she created in her kitchen in Alexandria, Virginia, alongside her mom, Amy. We liked this salad so much that it is now a part of our regular lunch rotation.

Eliza told us that *Run Fast. Eat Slow.*, "really changed my life by helping me run faster and build a healthier relationship with food." The addicting Lemon Miso Dressing in book one inspired the digestion-enhancing Orange Miso Dressing poured generously over this salad (see page 184 for both dressing variations).

Eliza loves that this dish is high in protein from the edamame and almonds and filling enough to be a meal by itself. It takes effort to prepare but will stay fresh for school or work lunches all week long. **SERVES 4**

---

**1** In a large salad bowl, combine the kale with three-quarters of the dressing and massage to soften the leaves.

**2** Add the carrots, orange, edamame, almonds, and green onions (if using), and toss to combine. Add more dressing to taste (we recommend using all the dressing, since the salad will continue to soak it up as it sits).

**3** Cover and refrigerate until ready to serve. This salad will keep in an airtight container in the refrigerator for up to 5 days.

**GLUTEN-FREE // VEGAN**

# SOUTHWEST SALAD

*FOR A MIGHTY MEAL-SIZE SALAD*

**1 small head romaine lettuce, washed, dried, chopped**

**1 can (14.5 ounces) black beans, rinsed and drained**

**2 carrots, peeled and grated**

**1 red bell pepper, chopped**

**½ cup shredded or crumbled cheese (cojita, feta, cheddar, pepper Jack)**

**1 recipe for yogurt dressing (from Purple Cabbage Slaw, page 165)**

**1 teaspoon chili powder**

**Topping ideas: avocado, tortilla chips, pumpkin seeds (optional)**

The labels on packaged foods can be misleading. For example, with salad dressing it might say, "Made with extra-virgin olive oil" on the front, but flip over to read the ingredients, and you'll find that the main oil is a cheap, inflammatory oil like canola or soybean oil.

Shalane and Elyse's fave salad from the Nike campus cafeteria in Beaverton, Oregon, inspired this recipe. Devour this Tex-Mex style salad as a main dish and you won't go hungry, thanks to the protein-packed beans and pumpkin seeds and the healthy fats from the yogurt dressing and avocado. Or up the ante and top it with leftover grilled chicken or steak.

To keep the lettuce crisp, only toss the portion that you'll be eating right away with dressing. To save time, you can use a creamy store-bought dressing, but check the label (see note below)—many bottled dressings are made with cheap vegetable oils and sugar. **SERVES 4**

**1** In an extra-large salad bowl, combine the lettuce, beans, carrots, pepper, and cheese.

**2** In a small bowl, prepare the dressing and whisk in the chili powder. Just before serving, toss the salad with three-quarters of the dressing. Taste and add the remaining dressing, if needed. Generously top the salad with sliced avocado, smashed tortilla chips, and pumpkin seeds, if desired.

**GLUTEN-FREE // VEGETARIAN // VEGAN:** Create a dairy-free version of this salad by tossing it with Creamy Cashew Dressing (Tex-Mex variation, page 180) instead of the yogurt dressing. And substitute Kalamata olives for the cheese.

# CAULIFLOWER TABBOULEH

*FOR FIGHTING INFLAMMATION*

1 large head cauliflower

3 cups loosely packed fresh herbs (any combo of parsley, basil, mint, cilantro)

1 pint cherry tomatoes, halved

4 green onions (scallions), white and green parts, sliced

3 tablespoons lemon juice (about 1 lemon)

2 tablespoons extra-virgin olive oil

¼ teaspoon fine sea salt

¼ teaspoon ground pepper

½ cup chopped walnuts or almonds (optional)

½ cup crumbled feta (optional)

This salad takes a little love to prepare. Plan ahead. The next time you're roasting cauliflower as a side dish, roast a double batch and use the leftovers to make this salad later in the week. It can also be made with 2 cups cooked grains such as quinoa, bulgur, couscous, or freekah instead of the cauliflower.

Don't let cauliflower's white color make you think it's any less nutritious. Cauliflower is rich in disease-fighting phytonutrients and antioxidants. And surprisingly, it's one of the most vitamin C–rich foods. There are also colorful varieties of cauliflower like purple and yellow, which are rich in antioxidants.

We created this grain-free variation of one of our favorite Mediterranean salads to sneak more veggies into family dinner. Get sneaky with cauliflower—pulse it in a food processor and it transforms into a couscous-like consistency. Even the pickiest of eaters will discover a newfound love for this cruciferous star.

This salad has workout recovery superpowers, thanks to the potent anti-inflammatory compounds in the fresh herbs and olive oil. It's the perfect accompaniment to summer grilling or can be transformed into a satisfying lunch by topping it with nuts and feta. **SERVES 4**

1  Roast the cauliflower according to the Simply Roasted Vegetables directions on page 159 but reduce the cook time to 20 to 25 minutes, to keep it crisp. Set aside to cool.

2  In a food processor or high-speed blender, briefly pulse the herbs until chopped and place in a salad bowl. Once the cauliflower has completely cooled, pulse it until finely chopped, and add it to the bowl.

3  Add the tomatoes, green onions, lemon juice, oil, salt, and pepper. Toss until combined. Taste and add more salt and pepper, if needed. Top with the nuts and cheese (if using).

4  Cover and chill in the fridge for at least 1 hour prior to serving.

**GLUTEN-FREE // VEGAN**

# SWEET POTATO SALAD
## FOR CARBO-LOADING IN STYLE

1 recipe Sunday Sweet Potatoes (about 3 cups) (page 161)

⅓ cup plain whole milk yogurt

1 tablespoon Dijon mustard

1 tablespoon lemon juice

¾ teaspoon fine sea salt

¼ teaspoon ground black pepper

1 cup shelled, thawed edamame

1 red bell pepper, chopped

½ cup chopped cilantro or parsley

2 tablespoons minced shallot or ¼ cup chopped green onion (scallions)

We use whole milk yogurt throughout this book in salads and dressings as a substitute for mayonnaise. We prefer yogurt because it provides a solid dose of probiotics, calcium, fat, and protein without the refined oils and sugar found in store-bought mayo. Many people who are sensitive to dairy do fine with adding a little yogurt to their diet, but if you're avoiding dairy completely, feel free to sub in a high-quality mayo or a non-dairy plain yogurt. If using mayo, reduce the salt in the recipe to half.

If you read our first cookbook, you know we have a serious love of sweet potatoes (yams) as the ultimate runner food. Sweet potatoes are an easily digestible source of complex carbs. So don't be surprised—we use sweet potatoes in everything from savory cakes (page 141) to waffles (page 82) to hummus (page 195) to energy foods (page 226).

This jazzed-up take on a picnic classic will have your friends clamoring for seconds at your next team dinner party or backyard BBQ.

The next time you roast a batch of Sunday Sweet Potatoes, double the recipe so you can quickly toss this salad together in time for a weekend picnic. **SERVES 5**

---

**1** Roast the sweet potatoes according to the recipe on page 161 and set aside to cool.

**2** In a large salad bowl, whisk together the yogurt, mustard, lemon juice, salt, and pepper. Add the sweet potatoes, edamame, red pepper, cilantro or parsley, and onion and toss.

**3** Taste and add more salt and pepper, if needed. Cover and chill in the fridge for at least 1 hour, or until ready to serve.

**GLUTEN-FREE // VEGETARIAN**

*"Do not go where the path may lead, go instead where there is no path and leave a trail."*

**–RALPH WALDO EMERSON**

# TOMATO MOZZARELLA SALAD

*FOR EASY SUMMER NIGHTS*

**4 vine-ripened or
2 heirloom tomatoes
(about 1 pound)**

**2 whole milk fresh
mozzarella balls
(4 ounces each)**

**2 tablespoons extra-virgin
olive oil**

**2 tablespoons balsamic
vinegar**

**Coarse sea salt**

**Black pepper**

**10 fresh basil leaves**

**Crusty bread**

Fresh herbs, like basil, are warriors for our bodies. They up our immune defenses, help combat stress, and reduce inflammation. Basil is easy to grow in a small pot on a windowsill.

Summer meals should be simple so that you can spend more time running and playing outside while the sunshine lasts. Let this refreshing, satisfying salad save the day. Make a meal out of it by serving it with a crusty baguette for soaking up the juices. For a protein-boost, add in a couple of hard-boiled eggs (see tip, page 93). Or serve it as a side with grilled fish or steak.

This salad should only be made when tomatoes are in season. Since grocery store tomatoes are flavorless, we highly recommend getting your tomatoes from the farmers' market. Bonus points if you grow your own backyard tomatoes and basil.

**SERVES 4**

**1** Thinly slice the tomatoes and mozzarella and arrange on a serving platter. Drizzle with the oil and vinegar and sprinkle generously with salt and pepper. (You don't really need to measure the oil and vinegar but we provided measurements for first timers.)

**2** Top with the basil (cut the basil into long strips by stacking and rolling the leaves and slicing along the roll).

**3** Serve with crusty bread for lapping up the juices.

**GLUTEN-FREE // VEGETARIAN**

# VEGGIE LOVER'S PASTA SALAD
## FOR A RAINBOW OF NUTRITION

½ box (8 ounces) penne or rotini pasta

1 head broccoli, cut into bite-size florets

4 packed cups (4 ounces) baby spinach

1 pint cherry tomatoes, halved (about 2 cups)

1 can (15 ounces) chickpeas (garbanzo beans), rinsed and drained

1 cup (4 ounces) crumbled feta

⅓ cup chopped Kalamata olives

1 recipe Lemon Miso Dressing (page 184)

When running pals are coming over for dinner, pasta salad and burgers are the ultimate in crowd-pleasing, easy party fare. Our revitalizing salad is packed with nutrient-dense veggies so you can feel good about devouring pasta for dinner.

Pasta salad need not be loaded with store-bought mayo made with cheap vegetable oil to be delicious. Toss it with our refreshing Lemon Miso Dressing (page 184) for a dose of anti-inflammatory olive oil and immune-boosting garlic.

This dish is a balanced meal on its own or serve as a side with Bonk Burgers (page 139) or Honey Balsamic Grilled Chicken (page 135). **SERVES 5**

**1**  Cook the pasta in heavily salted boiling water according to package directions. In the last 2 minutes of cook time, add the broccoli to the pot (turn up the heat to maintain at a boil). Place in a colander, rinse under cold water until chilled, and drain thoroughly.

**2**  In an extra-large salad bowl, combine the pasta, broccoli, spinach, tomatoes, garbanzo beans, feta, and olives. Add the dressing and toss to combine (we recommend using all of the dressing since the pasta will soak it up as it sits). Add salt and pepper to taste.

**3**  Cover and chill in the fridge for at least 1 hour, or until ready to serve. Leftovers will keep for up to 3 days.

**VEGETARIAN // GLUTEN-FREE:** This recipe can be easily made with gluten-free pasta or sub in boiled, chopped red potatoes and you've got a posh potato salad. // **DAIRY-FREE:** Leave out the cheese.

# PESTO TUNA MELT
## *FOR EASY-PEASY COMFORT FOOD*

1 can (5 ounces) tuna

⅓ cup pesto (see Presto Pesto, page 172)

1 tablespoon whole milk yogurt

4 slices whole-grain bread

4 slices cheese (cheddar, Gruyere, provolone, Gouda, etc.)

Olive oil for cooking

---

A true whole-wheat bread will have "whole-wheat flour" listed as the first ingredient not "wheat flour," which is the same as white flour. Look for sandwich breads with minimal ingredients and watch the sugar. Many whole-grain breads are loaded with sweeteners.

We runners sometimes just crave the simplicity of an ooey-gooey grilled cheese sandwich. When "hangry" symptoms set in and you need to eat pronto, make your grilled cheese worthy of the podium by stuffing it with zesty pesto tuna salad.

On chilly days, serve this sandwich with a cup of soup (Spring Asparagus Soup, page 119), and you've got it made. See page 92 for our recommendation on canned tuna brands to avoid harmful levels of mercury. **SERVES 2**

---

**1** In a medium bowl, combine the tuna, pesto, and yogurt.

**2** Place a slice of cheese on one piece of bread, spoon on the tuna mixture, cover with one more slice of cheese, and top it off with the remaining piece of bread.

**3** Heat a skillet over medium heat and drizzle with olive oil. Use a spatula to lower each sandwich into the pan. Drizzle oil on the top piece of bread. Grill until the bread gets nice and toasty. Carefully flip and grill the second side until the cheese is melted.

**GLUTEN-FREE:** Use gluten-free bread. **// DAIRY-FREE:** Sub in mayo or olive oil for the yogurt. Make vegan Presto Pesto (page 172) and skip the cheese.

# MEDITERRANEAN HUMMUS WRAP

## FOR A REVITALIZING LUNCH

### GREEK SALAD

2 cups peeled, chopped cucumber (about 2)

2 cups chopped tomato (about 2)

½ cup crumbled feta

¼ cup chopped, pitted Kalamata olives

2 tablespoons lemon juice or red wine vinegar

2 tablespoons extra-virgin olive oil

¼ teaspoon fine sea salt

¼ teaspoon ground pepper

### WRAP

4 whole-wheat pitas, wraps, or tortillas

1 cup Sweet Potato Hummus (page 195) or store-bought hummus

This refreshing Greek salad is super satisfying on a hot day. The hydrating combo of cucumbers and tomatoes mingles with the salty feta and olives to replenish sodium lost in a serious sweat session.

Wrap it all up in a tortilla with a slather of restorative Sweet Potato Hummus (page 195), and you've got a winning lunch (or dinner) fit for a pro. **SERVES 4**

1  In a medium bowl, combine the cucumber, tomato, feta, olives, lemon juice or vinegar, oil, salt, and pepper. Cover and refrigerate until ready to serve.

2  Warm the wrap by microwaving for 20 seconds. Smear generously with the hummus. Use a fork to fill with the salad (leaving the juices behind) and tightly roll up all the goodness.

3  The hummus and salad can be made in advance and stored for up to 5 days, but the wrap is best served just after filling to prevent soggy sadness.

**VEGETARIAN // GLUTEN-FREE:** Use gluten-free wraps or serve over salad greens. // **VEGAN/DAIRY-FREE:** Leave out the feta.

# 6 | DINNER BELL
# (AND SOUPS & SIDES)

# SUPERFOODS SOUP

*FOR SLURPING ENERGY*

2 tablespoons extra-virgin olive oil

2 carrots, peeled and diced

2 celery stalks, diced

1 yellow onion, diced

2 teaspoons fine sea salt

2 tablespoons curry powder

1 sweet potato (yam), unpeeled, cut ½-inch dice

1 can (13.5 ounces) unsweetened coconut milk

1 can (14.5 ounces) diced tomatoes

1 can (15 ounces) chickpeas (garbanzo beans)

3 cups chopped kale, stems removed

Juice of 1 lime

This mineral-rich, immune-boosting soup is loaded with nourishing whole foods, including sweet potatoes, chickpeas, and kale. But it's not just the rainbow of veggies that will give you a boost in this hearty Indian-inspired soup. The coconut milk has natural antiviral properties to help fend off cold and flu viruses. Plus the curry powder adds anti-inflammatory superpowers.

This recipe yields a lot because we like it a lot (you'll even find it featured in *The Runner's World Vegetarian Cookbook*). Freeze leftovers in individual portions for quick weeknight meals or mix things up the second night and serve leftovers over brown rice.

**SERVES 8**

---

**1**  Heat the oil in a large pot over medium-high heat. Add the carrots, celery, onion, and salt and cook, stirring occasionally, until softened but not brown, about 5 minutes. Add the curry powder and cook, stirring continuously, for 30 seconds, being careful not to let the spices brown.

**2**  Add 5 cups water, sweet potato, coconut milk, tomatoes, and chickpeas to the pot. Bring to a boil, then reduce the heat, and simmer covered, stirring occasionally, until the sweet potatoes are soft, about 20 minutes (be careful not to overcook).

**3**  Stir in the kale and simmer just until wilted. Turn off the heat and stir in 1 tablespoon of the lime juice. Taste and add more lime juice and salt, if needed.

**GLUTEN-FREE // VEGAN**

"It can be hard to get out the door on a cold, rainy day. To motivate me, I like to have everything prepared for dinner, especially a warm soup. Then I have something cozy and comforting to look forward to after I get the run done."

**—SHALANE**

# SLOW COOKER BEEF AND LENTIL MINESTRONE

*FOR DINNER AT THE READY*

2 tablespoons olive oil

1 pound ground beef (preferably grass-fed)

3 carrots, peeled and chopped

3 celery stalks, sliced

1 large yellow onion, chopped

2 teaspoons dried oregano

2 teaspoons fine sea salt (reduce in half if your broth is not low-sodium)

8 cups low-sodium vegetable broth

¾ cup green lentils, rinsed

1 can (14.5 ounces) diced tomatoes

3 cups chopped kale

Pasta, for serving

Parmesan, for serving (optional)

*\* Cook times with an Instant Pot can be misleading, since the pot needs time to come to pressure and to release. A large pot of soup will take about 20 minutes to come to pressure before the timer starts counting down. Think of it like an oven needing to preheat, but at least you don't need to watch over the pot.*

We snuck this hearty and nourishing soup recipe into the book as a late addition when Elyse realized she was making it nearly every week while in the midst of book edits and taking care of her new-born baby boy. If you, like us, find yourself in a constant scramble to get dinner on the table fast (before the fam gets too hangry!), this satisfying soup will become your new best friend.

Before you sprint out the door in the a.m., block out 15 minutes to toss this all together in your slow cooker or Instant Pot and you'll be greeted after a long day with delicious smells that will bring everyone to the table. **SERVES 6**

1  Set your slow cooker or Instant Pot to the sauté setting and add the oil and meat. Sauté until the meat begins to brown, using a wooden spoon to break into bite-size pieces, about 5 minutes. Add the carrots, celery, onion, oregano, and salt, and sauté for 5 minutes.

2  Add the broth, lentils, and tomatoes. Set the slow cooker to low for 8 hours or high for 4 hours. (Alternatively, if you're using an Instant Pot* this recipe can be cooked in 25 minutes using the manual high-pressure setting.)

3  Cook the pasta in a separate pot according to package directions. Drain and set aside.

4  Check that the lentils are soft. Just before serving, stir in the kale and cook until wilted. Taste and add salt and pepper, if needed.

5  Place a small serving of pasta in each soup bowl. Ladle the soup on top. Sprinkle with Parmesan (if using) and serve.

6  Store leftover pasta separately from leftover soup to prevent the pasta from soaking up all the broth.

**DAIRY-FREE // GLUTEN-FREE:** Skip the pasta—this soup can stand alone.

# CHICKEN CANNELLINI SOUP

**FOR SOOTHING THE SOUL (AND SORE MUSCLES)**

2 tablespoons extra-virgin olive oil

3 carrots, peeled and chopped

3 celery stalks, chopped

1 yellow onion, chopped

1¼ teaspoons fine sea salt (reduce in half if broth is not low-sodium)

4 garlic cloves, smashed

1 (32-ounce) box low-sodium chicken broth (or 4 cups homemade bone broth; see our first book)

1 pound skinless, boneless chicken thighs

1 can (15 ounces) cannellini beans (or other white bean), rinsed and drained

4 packed cups baby spinach

½ cup grated Parmesan (optional)

**Tummy troubles?** Sub in cooked rice instead of the beans and add a little fresh grated ginger.

**Hungry mob?** Double the recipe and stir cooked pasta or rice into each bowl.

Grandma's secret is tried and true—chicken soup can save the day. If you're fighting a cold or recovering from a taxing workout on a frigid day, this is the recipe to help you recruit your best defenses.

Broth is nourishing, hydrating, and soothing. Garlic and onions have antibacterial properties to help fight pesky germs, and the spinach and carrots are loaded with vitamin C. We prefer to use dark meat chicken, since it's more satiating and nutrient-dense than white.

Best part? With a little hustle, you can have a bowl of this steaming goodness on the table in 30 minutes. Ready. Set. Go!

**SERVES 4**

---

**1** Heat the oil in a large pot over medium heat. Add the carrots, celery, onion, and salt, and sauté until softened, about 5 minutes. Add the garlic and sauté for 1 minute.

**2** Add the broth, chicken, and beans. Bring to a boil, then turn the heat to low, and simmer covered for 20 minutes.

**3** Remove the chicken to a cutting board and use two forks to shred it into bite-size pieces. Return the chicken to the pot along with the spinach. Add salt and pepper to taste.

**4** Ladle into soup bowls and top with grated Parmesan (if using).

**GLUTEN-FREE // DAIRY-FREE**

# SPRING ASPARAGUS SOUP

**FOR SOUP IN THE SUMMERTIME**

2 tablespoons extra-virgin olive oil

2 leeks,* green tops removed, halved lengthwise, sliced

2 carrots, peeled and chopped

3 cloves garlic, smashed

1 teaspoon fine sea salt (cut in half if broth is not low-sodium)

4 cups low-sodium vegetable broth

1 bunch asparagus (about 1 pound), ends removed, quartered

2 small or 1 large zucchini, ends removed, diced

4 ounces soft goat cheese (chèvre)

1 tablespoon lemon juice

¼ teaspoon freshly ground black pepper

---

While you wait for this soup to simmer, try Shalane's Strength Routine on page 70.

*Can't find leeks? No problem. Sub in 1 yellow onion, chopped.*

If you loved the Broccoli Chèvre Soup in our first book, you'll fall hard for this refreshing variation that highlights spring and summer produce. Soup is super nourishing and hydrating and should have a home in your kitchen even during warmer months.

This recipe is a lifeline for families striving to eat more veggies. It's been tested and approved by the finicky little ones in our lives. **SERVES 5**

---

**1** Heat the oil in a large pot over medium-high heat. Add the leeks, carrots, garlic, and salt and cook, stirring occasionally, until the leeks begin to brown, about 5 minutes.

**2** Add the broth, asparagus, and zucchini. Bring to a boil, then reduce the heat to low. Simmer, covered, until the vegetables are tender, about 15 minutes. Turn off the heat and add the goat cheese, lemon juice, and pepper.

**3** If you have an immersion (stick) blender, use it to blend the soup right in the pot until smooth. Alternatively, allow the soup to cool slightly, then transfer it to a blender and process until smooth. Please note: Adding hot items to a blender causes the pressure to expand and can blow off the lid, so hold it firmly in place and blend on low.

**4** Taste and season with additional salt, pepper, and lemon juice, if needed.

**GLUTEN-FREE // VEGETARIAN // VEGAN:** Sub in 2 tablespoons tahini for the goat cheese and add more lemon juice to taste.

# BISON CHILI

## FOR KICKING IT UP A NOTCH

2 tablespoons extra-virgin olive oil

1 pound ground bison or ground beef (preferably grass-fed)

2 red bell peppers, chopped

1 large yellow onion, chopped

2 tablespoons chili powder*

1½ teaspoons fine sea salt

2 cans (15 ounces each) beans, rinsed and drained

1 can (15 ounces) tomato sauce (no sugar, no salt added)

1 can (14.5 ounces) fire-roasted, diced tomatoes

1 teaspoon ground cinnamon

⅛ teaspoon ground cayenne (optional), if you like it spicy

Topping ideas: avocado, sour cream, grated cheese, crumbled tortilla chips, and/or scallions

*Spices can vary a lot in quality. For the best flavor, buy your spices from a local spice shop that grinds them fresh in house.

We took our ever-popular Fartlek Chili recipe from our first book and broke it down into the essential parts to bring you the easiest chili recipe you'll ever make—without compromising fiery flavor. This is the ultimate comfort food to refuel after a long run on a dreary winter day.

Bison, from our favorite local ranch, is our iron-rich go-to, but feel free to sub in grass-fed ground beef, ground turkey, or crumbled tempeh. Use any combination of black beans, kidney beans, or pinto beans and don't forget the toppings. **SERVES 4**

---

1  Heat the oil in a large pot over medium-high heat. Add the meat and sauté until it begins to brown, using a wooden spoon to break into bite-size pieces, about 5 minutes. Add the peppers, onion, chili powder, and salt, and sauté for 5 minutes.

2  Add the beans, tomato sauce, tomatoes, ½ cup of water, cinnamon, and cayenne (if using). Bring to a boil. Turn the heat to low, cover, and simmer for 30 minutes, stirring occasionally.

3  Taste and add more salt, if needed, and cayenne (if using). If too thick, thin with a little more water.

4  Serve steaming hot topped with any combination of your favorite toppings.

5  Got leftovers? Serve on top of a steaming bowl of short-grain brown rice.

**GLUTEN-FREE // VEGAN:** Crumble 1 8-ounce package tempeh and sauté with the peppers and onions.

Vitamin C–rich foods help with iron absorption. This recipe is great for overcoming anemia, thanks to its combo of iron-rich red meat and vitamin C–loaded tomatoes.

**Got an Instant Pot?** This recipe can be cooked entirely in the Instant Pot by using the sauté setting to brown the meat and veggies. Then simply add the rest of the ingredients and set it to 20 minutes on manual high pressure. Or use the slow cooker setting to leave it simmering all day. See note on Instant Pot cook times, page 115.

"My kitchen is always a mess, but at least my family is eating a nourishing, home-cooked meal every night."

—ELYSE

# POWER BOWLS
## *FOR ENDLESS WHOLE BOWL GOODNESS*

Give an athlete a whole foods bowl, and you nourish him for a day. Teach an athlete to make nourishing bowls, and you feed him for a lifetime.

If you master only one recipe in this book, we hope it will be learning to make creative bowls. These one-dish meals are loaded with whole grains, veggies, protein, and satisfying sauces, making them our top pick for the ultimate runner food.

We've listed options for creating endless combos of nourishing bowls. Recipes within each step are listed in order of prep time, from fastest to more labor intensive. All of the sauces (except the guac) can be easily made ahead and frozen in individual portions for future bowls.

The photos on page 124 to 127 show our dream-worthy combos. We want to see yours! Tag your photos with #powerbowls and #runfasteatslow. **SERVES (VARIES)**

---

### STEP 1: **CHOOSE A BASE**

Our go-to for grain bowls is short-grain brown rice or quinoa. We highly recommend investing in a rice cooker or Instant Pot (see page 35). To lighten up your bowl or save time, salad greens, like baby spinach or arugula, also make a great base.

Salad greens

Quinoa (see cooking instructions, page 90)

Brown rice

Any whole grain: farro, freekah, barley, kamut, etc.

Coconut Rice with Nori, *page 164*

### STEP 2: **TOP WITH VEGGIES**

Top your bowl with a colorful rainbow of seasonal veggies to ensure you're getting a range of vitamins, minerals, antioxidants, fiber, and more.

Sliced avocado

Sautéed greens or Miso Fast Greens, *page 167*

Sunday Sweet Potatoes, *page 161*

Simply Roasted Vegetables, *page 159*

Leftover grilled veggies (try zucchini or asparagus)

Roasted Cauliflower and Potatoes, *page 162*

Purple Cabbage Slaw, *page 165*

Eat the Rainbow Stir-Fry, *page 142*

Tempeh Ratatouille, *page 158*

## STEP 3: ADD PROTEIN

Bowls can be a great way to use up leftovers. Every time you fire up the grill, cook extra meat or make enough of any of the below recipes to transform the leftovers into an enticing bowl. When in a time crunch, a fried egg saves the day.

Beans, chickpeas, or lentils

Fried egg (see cooking instructions, page 85)

Honey Balsamic Grilled Chicken, *page 135*

Crispy Tempeh, *page 143*

Miso Butter Salmon or Simply Broiled Salmon, *page 155*

Bonk Burger, *page 139*

Slow Cooker Pulled Pork or Chicken, *page 137*

## STEP 4: DRIZZLE SOME SAUCE

The sauce makes the meal. Sauces add not only an incredible burst of flavor (essential for satiation), but also a dose of healthy fats and inflammation-fighting spices.

We've created 6 crave-worthy sauces. Take your pick!

Creamy Ginger Cashew, *page 180*

Turmeric Coconut Curry, *page 181*

Garlicky Guac, *page 177*

Green Goddess Tahini, *page 178*

Pesto Yogurt, *page 175*

Smoky Summer Salsa, *page 176*

---

# SHALANE AND ELYSE'S FAVORITE BOWLS

### PULLED PORK BURRITO BOWL

>> Short-grain brown rice
>> Slow Cooker Pulled Pork/Chicken, *page 137*
>> Black beans
>> Purple Cabbage Slaw, *page 165*
>> Garlicky Guac, *page 177*
>> Cilantro

### GREEN ENVY RICE BOWL

>> Short-grain brown rice
>> Sautéed kale or Miso Fast Greens, *page 167*
>> Edamame
>> Sliced avocado
>> Green Goddess Tahini, *page 178*
>> Sesame seeds

### TEMPO QUINOA BOWL

>> Quinoa
>> Leftover Sunday Sweet Potatoes, *page 161*
>> Roasted Brussels sprouts (see Simply Roasted Vegetables, *page 159*)
>> Crispy Tempeh (*page 143*) or a fried egg
>> Creamy Ginger Cashew, *page 180*, or Turmeric Coconut Curry, *page 181*
>> Roasted cashews

### BURGER SALAD BOWL

>> Arugula or baby spinach
>> Grated carrot
>> Leftover Bonk Burger, *page 139*
>> Leftover grilled asparagus
>> Crumbled feta
>> Garlicky Guac, *page 177*, or Pesto Yogurt, *page 175*
>> Quick-Pickle Red Onions, *page 187*

**PULLED PORK
BURRITO BOWL**

GREEN ENVY RICE BOWL

TEMPO QUINOA BOWL

BURGER
SALAD
BOWL

# SHORTCUT PIZZA DOUGH

*FOR A WHOLESOME PIE*

**2 cups whole-wheat flour**

**1 cup all-purpose flour**

**1½ teaspoons fine sea salt**

**¼ teaspoon active dry yeast***

**1½ cups lukewarm water**

*\*You can find active dry yeast in the baking aisle at most grocery stores. It comes in small sealed envelopes. Once opened, store in the fridge for up to 3 months.*

There's an art and science to making perfect pizza dough that requires a scale, multiple risings, and lots of kneading. If you're in training mode, time is a precious commodity, so we came up with this easy-peasy dough that you don't have to touch while it rises.

You can buy freshly made pizza dough at many grocery stores, but with a whole-wheat dough recipe this simple there's really no need. Just be sure to plan ahead: This dough must be made 1 day in advance. **MAKES 2 PIES**

**1** In a large bowl, combine the flours (level with a knife to get an accurate measurement), salt, and yeast.

**2** Stir in the water and use your hands to briefly knead the dough just until it comes together (be careful not to overwork the dough). If the dough seems really dry, add another table-spoon of water.

**3** Divide the dough into 2 balls. Cover the bowl tightly with plastic wrap and leave at room temperature for 24 hours.

**4** After 24 hours, store dough in an airtight container in the fridge until ready to use. Dough will keep for up to 2 weeks in the fridge (slight discoloration is normal). Or place individual dough balls in a zipper bag and store in the freezer for up to 3 months.

**5** Ready to build your pizza? See pages 131 and 132 for instructions.

**VEGAN // DAIRY-FREE**

# QUINOA PIZZA CRUST

## FOR PIZZA THAT REPAIRS

**1½ cups leftover cooked quinoa (see cooking instructions, page 90)**

**1 egg**

**1 teaspoon dried oregano**

**1 teaspoon baking powder**

**¼ teaspoon fine sea salt**

**Topping ideas (see page 131)**

Quinoa is a superfood that works hard for your hardworking body. It's the only plant-based food that contains all nine essential amino acids (the building blocks of protein). It's also high in magnesium, an essential mineral for healthy bones, and iron, for cardiovascular strength.

This pizza doesn't have the chewy, doughy texture of a traditional crust, but it's surprisingly good. For best results, bake into small personal-size pizzas, since this style of crust is fragile.

**MAKES 2 8-INCH PIZZAS**

**1** Preheat the oven to 400°F. Line a baking sheet with parchment paper.

**2** In a medium bowl, combine the quinoa, egg, oregano, baking powder, and salt.

**3** Scoop the quinoa into two equal-size mounds on the baking sheet and use the back of a large spoon to spread out each crust into an 8-inch circle about ¼ inch thick.

**4** Bake in the oven for 25 minutes, or until firm in the center and golden.

**5** Add your favorite toppings (see pages 131 and 132 for inspiration) and bake for an additional 10 to 15 minutes. This pizza is best served right out of the oven, as it turns soggy by the next day.

**GLUTEN-FREE // VEGETARIAN // DAIRY-FREE**

# AMY'S RECOVERY PIZZA

*FOR ELITE-LEVEL PIZZA*

1 store-bought or homemade pizza dough (see Shortcut Dough, page 129, or Quinoa Crust, page 130)

1 tablespoon olive oil

1 cup pizza sauce (see Basic Pizza Sauce, page 182)

1 heaping cup leftover Sunday Sweet Potatoes (page 161)

4 ounces soft goat cheese (chèvre) or feta, crumbled

2 or 3 slices leftover cooked bacon, crumbled (optional)

1 egg (optional)

While at high-altitude training camp, the Bowerman Babes (Nike Elite Team) make homemade pizza and watch the *Bachelor* or *Bachelorette* together. It's a fun bonding night where they forget about the hard training! During spring training in Park City, they made Amy's Recovery Pizza every Monday.

*"Breathe out weakness and breathe in strength."*

**–AMY CRAGG**

Shalane's teammate and fellow Rio Olympic marathoner Amy Cragg inspired this gold medal pie. When we asked our fans on social media to vote on their favorite pizza toppings, we got a lot of awesome ideas, but nothing beat Amy's reply, "Sweet potatoes, goat cheese, bacon, and a fried egg in the middle!" Envisioning this sweet and salty flavor combo made our mouths water, so we set out to re-create it.

In college, Amy and her teammates would hit up a late night pizza joint after home meets. Her favorite pizza to indulge in was the "baked potato pizza." This is her grown-up version of that memorable slice. When Amy is in a pinch and doesn't have marinara sauce on hand, she subs in garlic butter. **SERVES 2**

**1** If your dough is refrigerated, leave it out for at least 1 hour to bring it up to room temperature. Preheat the oven to 500°F and oil your pizza stone or baking sheet with the olive oil.

**2** Generously flour a large cutting board. Form the dough into a ball, then use floured hands to stretch it as you rotate it until it's in a rough pizza shape. Lay on the cutting board and continue to pull and press to desired shape and thickness.

**3** Lay the dough centered on top of the pizza stone or baking sheet.

**4** Spread the sauce evenly over the dough, then top with the sweet potatoes, cheese, and bacon (if using). Put the egg in a small bowl.

**5** Place the pizza in the center of the oven and bake for 5 minutes. Carefully pull out the rack that the pizza is on and plop the egg in the center. Bake for an additional 7 to 8 minutes, or until the crust is golden and the white of the egg has set but the yolk is still runny. If skipping the egg, simply bake the pizza for 12 to 16 minutes.

**6** Slide pie back onto the cutting board and slice with a sharp knife.

**GLUTEN-FREE:** Quinoa Pizza Crust, page 130. // **VEGETARIAN:** Skip the bacon. // **DAIRY-FREE:** Skip the cheese.

# PIZZA CALI

**FOR A VEGGIE-LOADED PIE**

1 store-bought or homemade pizza dough (see Shortcut Dough, page 129, or Quinoa Crust, page 130)

2 tablespoons extra-virgin olive oil, divided

2 cups chopped broccoli

1 small zucchini, sliced into half moons (about 1 cup)

¾ cup pesto (see Presto Pesto, page 172)

Zest of ½ lemon

½ to ¾ cup crumbled feta or soft goat cheese (chèvre)

While on book tour, Shalane and Elyse shared many late-night meals together, including a memorable pizza dinner in San Francisco. That night Shalane exclaimed, "Write this pizza down in your phone so we can reinvent it for book two!" And then our version of what we came to call Pizza Cali was born.

The nourishing green veggies and refreshing lemon zest remind us of endless summer nights. Who knew pizza could be so vibrant and revitalizing? We know you'll love this pie as much as we do. **SERVES 3**

---

**1** If your dough is refrigerated, leave it out for at least 1 hour to bring it up to room temperature. Preheat the oven to 500°F and oil your pizza stone or baking sheet with about 1 tablespoon of the olive oil.

**2** In a medium bowl, toss the broccoli and zucchini with the remaining olive oil.

**3** Generously flour a large cutting board. Form the dough into a ball, then use floured hands to stretch it as you rotate it until it's in a rough pizza shape (oblong shapes are totally acceptable). Lay on the cutting board and continue to pull and press to the desired shape and thickness.

**4** Lay the dough centered on top of the pizza stone or baking sheet. Spread the pesto evenly over the dough. Top the pizza with the veggies, then the lemon zest, and finally the cheese.

**5** Place the pizza in the center of the oven and bake for 12 to 16 minutes, or until the edges are nicely browned.

**6** Slide pie back onto the cutting board and slice.

**VEGETARIAN** // **GLUTEN-FREE:** Quinoa Pizza Crust, page 130. // **DAIRY-FREE:** Hold the cheese and use vegan pesto.

# OVEN "FRIED" CHICKEN

## FOR A HEALTHY MAKEOVER

2 tablespoons olive oil

2 pounds skinless, boneless chicken (white and/or dark meat)

⅔ cup fine cornmeal (or all-purpose flour)

2 eggs

1 cup finely grated Parmesan cheese

1 cup almond meal

1 tablespoon dried oregano

¼ teaspoon fine sea salt

**Nut allergy?** Feel free to sub in bread-crumbs for the almond meal.

Going to college in the South meant we had our share of late night fried chicken. This recipe is reminiscent of those days, but with a healthy transformation so that we can feel good about serving it to our families. It's well worth the extra steps to bread skinless chicken prior to baking it, as it keeps the meat super moist and locks in flavor.

If you're following a gluten-free diet, you'll love this recipe. Instead of breadcrumbs, we use a satisfying combo of cornmeal and almond meal.

We like to make this with a mix of breasts and thighs to please the entire family, but feel free to use just one or the other.

**SERVES 4**

1  Preheat the oven to 425°F. Line a rimmed baking sheet with foil and smear with the oil. If using large chicken breasts, cut them in half. Pat the chicken dry and sprinkle generously with salt and pepper on all sides.

2  Line up three low-sided bowls on the counter. Place the cornmeal in the first bowl. Whisk the eggs in the second bowl. In the third bowl, combine the Parmesan, almond meal, oregano, and salt.

3  Dredge each piece of chicken first in the cornmeal, then in the eggs (shake off excess), and lastly in the Parmesan mixture to coat on all sides. Place the breaded chicken on the baking sheet. Discard the leftover breading.

4  Bake in the center of the oven until crispy on the outside and cooked through, about 20 to 25 minutes.

**GLUTEN-FREE**

# HONEY BALSAMIC GRILLED CHICKEN

**FOR PROTEIN PRONTO**

¼ cup balsamic vinegar

¼ cup extra-virgin olive oil

2 tablespoons honey

1 tablespoon Dijon mustard

½ teaspoon fine sea salt

2 pounds skinless, boneless chicken thighs

Grill up enough chicken for crave-worthy leftovers. Serve on top of DIY Grain Salads (page 95) or Power Bowls (page 122).

When Shalane visited Elyse in Bend on a summer weekend for our cookbook photo shoot, Elyse grilled this quick and flavorful marinated chicken. The dish was such a hit that it became a must-have addition to the cookbook. The honey-balsamic marinade forms a glaze on the chicken that locks in moisture and leads to delectable charred edges.

For grilling, we always stick to dark meat chicken, since it has a higher fat content and won't dry out. Plus, it's more nutrient dense than white meat and has a richer, more satiating flavor.

**SERVES 5**

**1** In a gallon-size freezer bag, combine the vinegar, oil, honey, mustard, and salt. Add the chicken, seal the bag, and massage to combine.

**2** Place in the fridge and allow the chicken to marinate for at least 4 hours or overnight.

**3** Remove the chicken from the fridge 30 minutes prior to grilling. Preheat the grill to medium-high. Use tongs to lift chicken from bag, shake off excess marinade, and carefully place on the grill (will flame up).

**4** Close the grill lid and cook for 3 to 4 minutes per side, or until nicely charred and the chicken is cooked through (165°F on an instant-read thermometer).

**5** If you don't have access to an outdoor grill, an indoor nonstick grill pan on the stovetop works well.

**6** For a showstopping meal, serve this chicken with our Southwest Salad (page 98).

**GLUTEN-FREE // DAIRY-FREE**

# SLOW COOKER PULLED PORK OR CHICKEN
## FOR MANY MEALS IN ONE

1 (3- to 4-pound) pork shoulder or 3 to 4 pounds skinless, boneless chicken thighs (not white meat)

1 onion, chopped

5 cloves garlic, roughly chopped

¼ cup apple cider vinegar

2 tablespoons soy sauce

2 tablespoons honey

2 chipotle peppers in adobe sauce (canned)*

1 tablespoon chili powder

2 tablespoons lime juice

*The chipotle peppers add a delicious smoky flavor and just the right amount of spice, but if your crowd is spice averse, simply leave them out. Alternatively, if you love spice but your kids do not, you can leave them in but remove a serving of the meat for the kiddos before you simmer the remaining meat in the sauce. Freeze leftover chipotle peppers spread out in a quart-size zipper bag to make it easy to break off just the amount needed.*

Shalane made this recipe frequently while training for both the 2017 NYC Marathon and the 2018 Boston Marathon, since she could count on it for several meals with rice and veggies.

This recipe takes a little love to prepare but is well worth the effort, since it results in awesome-sauce leftovers that can be repurposed in imaginative ways.

What creative ways, you say? Serve on top of corn tortillas with Garlicky Guac (page 177) and cilantro. Pile onto rice with Purple Cabbage Slaw (page 165) and sliced avocado. Use as the ultimate topping for baked potatoes. Serve on top of your favorite salad or stuff into a baguette for a mouthwatering pulled-pork sandwich. **SERVES 8**

**1** Sprinkle the pork or chicken generously on all sides with salt and pepper.

**2** Add the onion, garlic, ½ cup water, vinegar, soy sauce, honey, chipotle peppers, and chili powder to the slow cooker. Stir to combine and submerge the meat in the liquid.

**3** Set your slow cooker to high for 5 hours or low for 8 hours (chicken cooks faster than pork and can be ready in 3 hours on high).

**4** Use tongs to carefully remove the meat to a large plate (do not toss out the juices) and use two forks to shred. Break up the chipotle peppers. Return the meat to the slow cooker. Cook for 1 more hour to allow the meat to absorb the flavors from the juices (if you have a lot of liquid left, you can simmer with the lid off to concentrate the flavors).

**5** Turn off the heat and stir in the lime juice. Taste and add more soy sauce or lime juice, if needed. If serving on tacos, use a slotted spoon.

**6** Leftovers should be transferred to a glass container, cooled briefly, covered, and stored in the fridge. Never leave cooked meat sitting out at room temperature.

**GLUTEN-FREE // DAIRY-FREE**

# CHIPOTLE BLACK BEAN BURGERS
## FOR VEGETARIAN BURGER BLISS

1 tablespoon virgin coconut oil, plus more for frying

1 cup finely chopped onion

1 teaspoon fine sea salt, divided

2 cans (14.5 ounces each) black beans, rinsed and drained

½ cup oat flour*

1 egg

2 chipotle peppers in adobe sauce (canned), chopped (see page 139 for storage tip)

2 tablespoons tahini (ground sesame seeds)

1 teaspoon ground cumin

1 lime, cut into wedges

*You can buy oat flour or make your own by pulsing rolled oats in a blender or food processor until finely ground. We use oat flour throughout this book, so we recommend pulsing a few cups at a time so that you have it at the ready.

Stock these burgers in your freezer for quick weeknight meals. Wrap them individually or stack them with parchment paper between layers. Thaw overnight and reheat in the microwave.

These are the burgers you make when you want to impress your vegetarian friends. The chipotle peppers add a smoky flavor reminiscent of backyard BBQs. Frying them in coconut oil results in a crispy exterior—say goodbye to soggy, frozen veggie burgers.

No buns, hon. Simply dress them up with a squeeze of fresh lime juice or slather them in Garlicky Guac (page 177). For a complete dinner menu, serve with a side of Sunday Sweet Potatoes (page 161) and Purple Cabbage Slaw (page 165). Or serve on salad greens topped with a fried egg, sliced avocado, and pickled onions (page 187). **MAKES 8 BURGERS**

**1**  Heat the oil in a frying pan or cast-iron skillet over medium-high heat. Add the onions and ½ teaspoon of the salt and cook until softened, about 5 minutes. Remove the pan from the heat.

**2**  Dry the beans well with a paper towel, place in a large bowl, and use a potato masher (or your hands) to smash until sticky with some whole pieces.

**3**  Add the cooked onion, oat flour, egg, peppers, tahini, cumin, and remaining ½ teaspoon of salt to the beans and stir well to combine. To firm up, place mixture in the fridge for 15 minutes—or until ready to fry.

**4**  Heat the same pan (wipe it clean with a towel) over medium heat. Add enough coconut oil to completely coat the bottom. Use a ⅓ measuring cup to scoop the burgers into the pan, being careful not to overcrowd them. Flatten slightly with a spatula. Cook for 4 minutes, or until golden and crispy. Carefully flip each burger and cook for an additional 3 to 4 minutes.

**5**  Transfer to a paper towel–lined plate. Carefully wipe out the pan, add more oil, and continue with the remaining burgers. Serve the burgers with lime wedges.

**GLUTEN-FREE // VEGETARIAN // DAIRY-FREE**

# BONK BURGERS

*FOR PREVENTING FATIGUE*

**1 pound ground beef or bison (preferably grass-fed)**

**1 egg**

**¼ cup chopped parsley**

**¼ cup oat flour or almond flour***

**2 cloves garlic, minced, or ½ teaspoon garlic powder**

**½ teaspoon fennel seeds (optional; see note below)**

**½ teaspoon fine sea salt**

**¼ teaspoon ground black pepper**

**5 pitas or whole-wheat rolls (optional)**

*\*You can buy oat flour or make your own by pulsing rolled oats in a blender or food processor until finely ground.*

 Fennel seeds contain a concentrated source of minerals and are great for digestion. Try chewing a few fennel seeds after a heavy meal or steep them with hot water to make a tea.

Hungry fam? Double the recipe so you have leftovers for Burger Bowls (page 123). You can also crumble leftover burgers into marinara sauce for bolognese in an instant.

Red meat is a great source of protein, healthy fats, energizing B vitamins, and blood-building iron. Buy the highest quality red meat for maximum flavor and nutrition. Many grocery stores now offer grass-fed ground beef. Better yet, buy your meat direct from a local farmer. We like to keep the seasonings simple to let the meat shine.

Endurance athletes can suffer from fatigue due to low iron. Since exercise depletes iron stores, runners need more iron in their diet than the average person. In our homes, we cook burgers on a weekly basis. **MAKES 5 BURGERS**

---

**1** Remove the meat from the fridge 30 minutes prior to cooking to bring it up to room temperature.

**2** Preheat the grill to medium-high.

**3** In a large mixing bowl, combine the egg, parsley, flour, garlic, fennel (if using), salt, and pepper. Add the meat and use your hands to combine, being careful not to overwork it. Form into 5 equal-size patties about 1 inch thick.

**4** Grill the burgers, flipping once, until a thermometer inserted in the center registers 160°F and the meat is no longer pink, 3 to 4 minutes per side. In the last minute, warm the pitas or rolls on the grill (if using).

**5** We love these burgers topped with Garlicky Guac (page 177), Green Goddess Tahini Sauce (page 178), or Sweet Potato Hummus (page 195).

**DAIRY-FREE // GLUTEN-FREE:** Serve the burgers in lettuce wraps.

# SWEET POTATO CHICKPEA CAKES
## FOR SATISFYING FRIED-FOOD CRAVINGS

1 can (14.5 ounces) chickpeas (garbanzo beans), rinsed and drained

1 cup cooked, mashed sweet potato (yams, not canned) *

½ cup rolled oats

½ yellow onion, finely diced

½ cup minced fresh parsley

2 eggs, beaten

1 teaspoon ground cumin

¾ teaspoon fine sea salt

¼ teaspoon freshly ground black pepper

¼ to ½ cup coconut oil or other high-heat oil, for frying

1 lemon or lime, cut into wedges

*To bake sweet potatoes, wrap 2 (1 to 1½ pounds) orange-fleshed sweet potatoes (yams) in foil. Bake at 400°F until tender, 45 to 60 minutes. Cool, remove the skin, and mash by hand with a fork until smooth. Can be baked up to 3 days in advance. Two medium yams makes 1 cup mashed.

Shalane's fave recipe in book numero uno is the Salmon Sweet Potato Cakes, so we had to craft another savory cake, with beloved sweet potatoes as the base.

To save you time and money, we opted for a vegetarian variation, but these cakes still pack a mean punch of vitamins and protein. They're fried until crispy, and you shouldn't fear the fat. We use virgin coconut oil for its host of health benefits (see page 55). **MAKES 20 SMALL CAKES**

---

**1** Place the chickpeas in a large bowl and use a fork to smash them thoroughly into pieces. Add the sweet potato, oats, onion, parsley, eggs, cumin, salt, and pepper and stir to combine. Let the mixture rest for 15 minutes in the fridge to firm up.

**2** Heat a frying pan or cast-iron skillet over medium-high heat. Add enough oil to generously coat the bottom of the pan. Scoop a heaping tablespoon of batter into the skillet and press down lightly with a spatula to flatten. Continue with remaining batter being careful not to overcrowd the pan.

**3** Cook cakes for 2 to 3 minutes, or until golden brown (don't flip too soon or they'll fall apart). Flip cakes and cook for an additional 2 minutes. Transfer to a paper towel–lined baking sheet or plate.

**4** Carefully wipe out the pan, add more oil, and continue frying the remaining batter.

**5** Cakes can be reheated in the oven at 275°F until warm. Serve as an appetizer on a platter garnished with lemon or lime wedges.

**6** Store leftover cakes in the fridge for up to 5 days or in the freezer for up to 3 months.

**GLUTEN-FREE:** Use certified gluten-free oats. // **VEGETARIAN** // **DAIRY-FREE**

# EAT THE RAINBOW STIR-FRY

**FOR UPPING YOUR VEG PROFILE**

### MARINADE

8 ounces skinless chicken, chopped

2 tablespoons soy sauce

1 tablespoon lime juice

1 tablespoon honey

1 tablespoon minced garlic and/or ginger

### VEGGIES

2 tablespoons high-heat oil (like safflower, sesame, or avocado oil)

½ large or 1 small yellow onion, sliced

2 heaping cups chopped hard vegetables (carrots, celery, broccoli)

1 heaping cup sliced soft vegetables (snap peas, bell pepper, cabbage, bok choy, mushrooms)

We rely on a weekly stir-fry to help us use up a leftover odd assortment of veggies. In this recipe, choose your own adventure, but aim for a range of colors to max out the nutrition potential.

There is an art and science to stir-frying in style. Here are a few tips.

>> Prep all the ingredients before you start frying. Chop veggies to similar sizes so they cook evenly.

>> Get the pan really hot and keep it hot.

>> Don't walk away. Stir-frying means quick cooking over high heat with frequent stirring.

>> Keep excess moisture out of the pan. Dry your veggies after washing them and add the sauce last.

>> Cook hard vegetables first and soft, moisture-rich ingredients last.

Don't crowd the pan. If you have a lot of veggies and meat, cook them separately and then combine at the end. **SERVES 2**

---

**1** Place the chicken, soy sauce, lime juice, and honey in a quart-size zipper bag and shake to combine. Leave out for 20 minutes to allow meat to marinate and come up to room temperature (for even more flavor marinate overnight in the fridge).

**2** Heat a wok or high-sided sauté pan over high heat. Add the oil, onion, and hard vegetables. Cook, stirring frequently, until the veggies begin to brown, about 5 minutes.

**3** Turn the heat down to medium-high, add the soft vegetables, and sauté for 2 minutes. Add the chicken with the marinade and sauté, stirring occasionally, until the chicken is cooked through, about 5 minutes.

**4** Use a clean spoon to serve on top of brown rice or quinoa and drizzle with your favorite spicy sauce like sriracha, Turmeric Coconut Curry Sauce (page 181), or Creamy Ginger Cashew Sauce (page 180).

**DAIRY-FREE // GLUTEN-FREE // VEGETARIAN:** Leave out the chicken, add in more veggies and/or beans, and add the marinade toward the end of sautéing.

# CRISPY TEMPEH
## FOR MEATLESS MONDAY

1 (8 ounce) package tempeh, cut into 1-inch squares

⅓ cup soy sauce

3 cloves garlic, smashed

2-inch piece ginger, peeled, sliced

Virgin coconut oil (or other high-heat oil), for frying

We aren't huge fans of tofu because it's highly processed, lacks the nutrients found in whole soybeans, and can be difficult to digest. Instead we want you to reach for tofu's lesser-known star sister, tempeh. Tempeh is made from whole, fermented soybeans, making it rich in probiotics, easy to digest, and high in protein.

Tempeh is essential for vegans, since it contains B vitamins, calcium, and iron. Studies show it is amazing for muscle recovery and bone density. This superstar food requires a little love to make it taste great, and this easy recipe does the trick. Try it served on top of a Power Bowl (page 122). **SERVES 3**

**1** Place the tempeh in a medium saucepan with 1½ cups water, soy sauce, garlic, and ginger. Bring to a boil, reduce the heat, cover, and simmer for 30 minutes.

**2** Use a colander to drain the tempeh thoroughly and discard the marinade.

**3** Heat a cast-iron skillet or frying pan over medium-high heat. Add enough oil to generously coat the bottom of the pan and, once shimmering, carefully place the tempeh in the oil. Pan-fry both sides for 3 minutes, or until golden and crispy. Transfer to a plate lined with paper towels until ready to serve.

**VEGAN // GLUTEN-FREE**

# MARATHON BOLOGNESE
### FOR A SAUCE THAT SUSTAINS

1 tablespoon extra-virgin olive oil

1 pound ground beef or bison (preferably grass-fed)

1 teaspoon fine sea salt, divided

3 cloves garlic, minced

2 teaspoons dried oregano

½ teaspoon red pepper flakes (optional)

2 red bell peppers, seeded and chopped

2 heaping cups sliced mushrooms

1 can (28 ounces) crushed or diced tomatoes*

4 cups baby spinach or chopped kale (optional)

Parmesan (optional)

*It's worth paying a little extra for a high-quality brand of canned tomatoes to get a sweet result. If your sauce tastes too acidic, add a teaspoon or two of sugar.

 **Mix It Up:** This sauce is also delicious with carrots, celery, and onions instead of the garlic, peppers, and mushrooms.

If you have a small amount of sauce left over, freeze it for home-made pizza night.

Traditional bolognese is heavy on the beef and skimpy on the veggies. We prefer our sauce to be veg-loaded to maximize flavor and nutrition. The first time you make this sauce, try it with the enticing combo below, but once you've mastered sauce making, experiment by using any assortment of your favorite veggies.

We love our pasta as much as the next runner and like this sauce best on top of spaghetti. But if you're following a gluten-free diet, it's also delicious over brown rice or roasted spaghetti squash. **SERVES 4**

---

**1** Heat the oil in a large pot over medium-high heat. Add the beef and ½ teaspoon of the salt and cook until lightly browned, stirring frequently while breaking up the meat into bite-size pieces, about 3 minutes. Add the garlic, oregano, and red pepper flakes (if using), and sauté for 1 minute.

**2** Add the bell peppers, mushrooms, and remaining ½ teaspoon of the salt (if your meat is lean, add another tablespoon of oil). Cook, stirring occasionally, until the mushrooms soften, about 5 minutes.

**3** Add the tomatoes. Bring to a boil, reduce heat to a simmer, and cook uncovered, stirring occasionally, until the sauce thickens, about 25 minutes. Stir in the spinach or kale (if using).

**4** Taste and add more salt and pepper, if needed.

**5** Serve over pasta, rice, zucchini noodles, or spaghetti squash and top with grated Parmesan (if using).

**GLUTEN-FREE // DAIRY-FREE:** Skip the Parmesan.

*"F&@# yeah!!"*
**—SHALANE** ☺

# TURKEY TROT MEATBALLS

## FOR REVIVING SORE MUSCLES

1 tablespoon olive oil

½ cup finely grated Parmesan

⅓ cup almond flour or oat flour (see tip, page 138)

¼ cup finely chopped parsley

½ teaspoon garlic powder

½ teaspoon fine sea salt

¼ teaspoon ground black pepper

1 pound ground turkey

1 egg

---

We left the seasoning in these meatballs simple to appeal to kids and kids-at-heart. If you want to dress them up, add ½ teaspoon fennel seeds and ¼ teaspoon red pepper flakes.

While marathon training, Shalane likes to make these meatballs with grass-fed beef or bison for an extra iron boost.

Homemade meatballs steal our hearts (as you can tell from the cover of this book!). These turkey meatballs are a constant in our kitchens. They are crispy and snack-able right out of the oven and next level simmered in sauce and served over spaghetti. Or serve them as a high-protein appetizer with a side of marinara for dunking.

If you're hooked on processed turkey deli meat, try these as a replacement. Leftover meatballs are great in a sandwich or on a salad or rice bowl. Gobble-gobble your turkey to get your fix of energizing B vitamins and muscle-building protein. **SERVES 4**

---

**1** Preheat the oven to 400°F. Line a baking sheet with parchment paper and drizzle the oil across the paper (use your fingers to spread evenly).

**2** In a large bowl, combine the Parmesan, flour, parsley, garlic powder, salt, and pepper. Add the turkey and egg and use your hands to combine. Set aside for 15 minutes to absorb moisture.

**3** Use a spoon to scoop and your hands to form the meat into golf-ball sizes, about 16 total meatballs. Place the meatballs evenly spaced on the prepared baking sheet.

**4** Bake in the center of the oven for 15 minutes. Remove from the oven, flip each meatball, and return to the oven for 15 minutes, or until the meatballs are crispy and lightly browned. Cut open a meatball to check for doneness (no pink).

**5** Optional: Simmer in our Basic Pizza Sauce (page 182) for 30 minutes, until the sauce thickens or heat your favorite marinara sauce, add the meatballs, and serve on top of pasta.

**GLUTEN-FREE:** Use almond flour and serve on gluten-free pasta. //
**DAIRY-FREE:** Skip the Parmesan.

# PESTO PASTA WITH SARDINES
## *FOR BRAIN-BOOSTING OMEGA-3S*

**8 ounces (½ box) spaghetti (or penne pasta)**

**1 tablespoon extra-virgin olive oil**

**4 cups baby spinach**

**1 cup pesto (see Presto Pesto, page 172)**

**1 tin (4.4 ounces) sardines in olive oil, drained**

**Fine sea salt (optional)**

**Ground black pepper (optional)**

Elyse's daughter Lily's three favorite foods are sardines (true story!), pesto, and pasta. When Elyse decided to combine all her favorites into one dish, this pasta came to be and is now a steadfast regular on our table.

Trust us on the sardines. When paired with pesto, they're mild and not at all fishy. Sardines are an incredibly nutritious food. They're loaded with protein, are one of the best sources of omega-3 fatty acids, and are high in essential nutrients for athletes, including vitamin B12, vitamin D, calcium, and iron.

Bonus: Sardines are a sustainable fish and are free from contaminants such as mercury, so they're safe to eat on a regular basis. Of course, if you're still fearful of these little guys, feel free to sub in canned tuna. Just be sure to buy a high-quality brand like Safecatch or Wild Planet to avoid harmful levels of mercury.

**SERVES 3**

---

**1** Cook the pasta in generously salted boiling water according to the package directions. Prior to draining, reserve about ¼ cup of the pasta cooking water.

**2** Return the pot to the stove over low heat, add the olive oil and spinach, and cook just until wilted. Add the pesto, sardines, and a splash of the pasta cooking water and use tongs to toss. If needed, add a little more pasta water just until the pesto coats the pasta.

**3** Taste and add salt and pepper, if needed.

**GLUTEN-FREE:** This dish is stellar made with zucchini noodles, aka zoodles! // **DAIRY-FREE:** Use the vegan variation of our pesto (page 172).

# GET BETTER ZZZZZZZ'S

While on our book tour together, we shared many hotel rooms across the country from San Francisco to Chicago to NYC to Chapel Hill. One thing that impressed Elyse—almost as much as Shalane's marathon pace (5:23 per mile!)—was her sleep habits. Shalane could fall asleep in minutes (despite a 3-hour time change), while Elyse would lie wide-awake in bed for hours.

Shalane also taught Elyse the art of napping. On our first book tour stop in Seattle, in between multiple events, Shalane managed to find time in the middle of the afternoon to get us back to the hotel room for a snooze. Elyse couldn't remember the last time she laid down in the middle of the day.

Sleep is just as important for recovery as nutrition. Here are our top sleep tips.

**1** >> Endurance athletes should get 8 to 10 hours of sleep per night.

**2** >> Keep a consistent schedule. (Shalane goes to bed at 9 p.m. and gets up around 6 a.m.) This helps your body establish a circadian rhythm to maximize deep REM sleep (the kind of sleep that repairs the body).

**3** >> Rise early and get outside first thing in the a.m. to set your body clock (and circadian rhythm).

**4** >> Avoid caffeine after 12:30 p.m. Sorry, no afternoon coffee break! Green tea is a great option if you need a light pm caffeine boost (or a square of dark chocolate!).

**5** >> Keep daytime naps to under an hour to avoid affecting nighttime sleep. Naps for Shalane are more about decompressing. You don't have to actually fall asleep to benefit from a power nap.

**6** >> Turn off your phone (and other electronics) an hour before bed. Research shows the light that illuminates from devices keeps our brains from being able to slow down. Read a few pages of a mindless book in bed (nothing too juicy!) to quiet your mind.

**7** >> Believe in the hard work you put in. Don't dwell on anything negative while in bed. If you can't stop thinking about a stressful to-do list, keep pen and paper by your bed and jot down thoughts to get them out of your head.

**8** >> Relax with a cup of herbal tea and a light snack before bed. See Best Bedtime Snacks (page 201).

# HOMESTYLE MAC AND CHEESE WITH BROCCOLI
## FOR HEARTY COMFORT FOOD

1 box (1 pound) elbow macaroni or fusilli

1 large head broccoli, cut into bite-size florets

2½ cups (8 ounces) grated sharp cheddar cheese

1½ cups (5 ounces) grated Gruyere cheese (or Colby cheese)

½ cup whole milk

2 tablespoons butter

½ teaspoon fine sea salt

Ground black pepper, to taste

While on our book tour in North Carolina, we received several requests for a homemade mac and cheese recipe. Not surprisingly, the first two recipes Shalane and her husband, Steve, decided to recipe test were this decadent mac and cheese and our Oven "Fried" Chicken (page 134). Both recipes were a hit and are now on tap in the Flanagan household.

Sure, you could buy boxed mac and cheese for a fraction of the cost, but powdered cheese is highly processed, and recent research shows it may be high in harmful chemicals. Plus, once you taste this homestyle version made with real cheese, you'll never go back. It's surprisingly easy to make from scratch and will satisfy both kids and kids-at-heart.

This recipe is party-size. Feel free to cut it in half if you're feeding a smaller group. **SERVES 8**

---

**1**  In a large pot, cook the pasta according to the package directions until al dente (it will keep cooking in the sauce). In the last 2 minutes of boiling, add the broccoli to the same pot. Drain the pasta and broccoli thoroughly and return to the pot.

**2**  Turn the heat to low. Add the cheeses, milk, butter, salt, and pepper and stir until the cheese melts. If dry, add another splash of milk until the sauce is creamy. Taste and season with more salt and pepper, if needed. Serve immediately to prevent the cheese from clumping.

**VEGETARIAN**

# BROWN RICE RISOTTO WITH MUSHROOMS AND PEAS

*FOR DATE-NIGHT DINNERS*

2 tablespoons unsalted butter or olive oil

3 cups sliced mushrooms

1 yellow onion, diced

3 cloves garlic, smashed

¾ teaspoon fine sea salt (reduce to ¼ teaspoon if broth is not low-sodium)

3 cups low-sodium vegetable broth (or low-sodium chicken broth)

1 cup short grain brown rice

1 cup grated Parmesan cheese

1 cup frozen peas, thawed

Grated zest of 1 lemon (about 1 tablespoon; optional)

2 tablespoons lemon juice

¼ teaspoon ground black pepper

¼ cup chopped fresh herbs (basil, mint, parsley; optional)

Traditional risotto requires standing over the stove and continuously stirring while adding a little bit of broth at a time. With this risotto recipe, we've rebelled against the classic technique to bring you a fuss-free and more nutritious risotto made with brown rice.

This dish can be served as a complete vegetarian meal in itself—even better topped with a fried egg. Or put on your fancy pants and serve it as a side dish with grilled steak or fish.

Leave the rice to simmer untouched for 45 minutes, and you have just enough time to complete Shalane's strength training routine (see page 70). Ready, steady, go! **SERVES 4**

1 Melt the butter or olive oil in a large pot with a lid over medium-high heat. Add the mushrooms, onion, garlic, and salt and cook, stirring occasionally, until softened, about 5 minutes.

2 Add the broth and rice and bring to a boil. Reduce the heat to low and simmer covered for 45 minutes (no need to stir).

3 Remove the lid and simmer uncovered, stirring occasionally, for 15 to 20 minutes, or until excess liquid evaporates (leave just enough liquid to keep the rice creamy).

4 Stir in the Parmesan, peas, lemon zest (if using), lemon juice, and pepper. Just before serving, stir in the herbs (if using).

**GLUTEN-FREE // VEGETARIAN**

# MISO BUTTER SALMON

**FOR AN OMEGA BOOST**

**1 pound salmon fillet (preferably wild)***

**¼ teaspoon fine sea salt**

**2 tablespoons Miso Honey Butter (page 183)**

**Sesame seeds (optional)**

*\*Salmon is very easy to over-cook, since it continues to cook from residual heat after you remove it from the oven. Check it after 10 minutes in the thickest portion of the fillet and, if close to done, remove from oven, wrap the foil around it, and allow to rest for 10 minutes.*

Leftover miso butter will keep in the fridge for up to 2 weeks. Just be sure not to cross-contaminate by dipping the spoon that touched the raw fish into the butter.

While in training mode (Shalane) or pregnant (Elyse), we crave salmon like it's chocolate. Must be because it's loaded with energizing vitamin B12, anti-inflammatory omega-3 fatty acids, bone-building vitamin D, and of course, muscle-building protein, all ideal for recovery (and growing a baby!).

Lucky for us, here in Oregon we're blessed with access to wild chinook and coho salmon. Wild salmon, while expensive, is worth the price. It's much better for the environment and your hard-working body. Other equally delicious substitutes include black cod, arctic char, and steelhead. **SERVES 4**

**1** Preheat the oven to 425°F and line a baking sheet with foil.

**2** Place the salmon skin-side down on the baking sheet and sprinkle with the salt. Use an offset spatula or spoon to smear the miso butter on top of the fillet. The butter doesn't need to be spread out perfectly; just coat the fish as best as you can.

**3** Bake in the center of the oven for 10 to 16 minutes (depending on thickness), or until opaque in the center of the fish.

**4** Garnish with sesame seeds (if using) and serve immediately with brown rice or Sunday Sweet Potatoes (page 161).

### SIMPLY BROILED SALMON

Position an oven rack 3 to 4 inches from the broiler and turn on broil. Place the salmon skin-side down on a baking sheet lined with aluminum foil. Sprinkle the salmon generously with salt and pepper and your favorite spices (we like a combo of smoked paprika and garlic powder). Drizzle with olive oil and rub in the spices.

Broil the salmon until it begins to char on the top and is opaque in the thickest portion, about 3 to 4 minutes. If your salmon filet is thick, flip it and cook it for another 3 to 4 minutes with the skin-side up.

**GLUTEN-FREE**

# BAKED FISH WITH GREEN BEANS AND TOMATOES

*FOR A REFRESHING SUMMER DINNER*

3 cups chopped bite-size green beans

1 pint cherry tomatoes

¼ cup chopped black olives or capers

3 tablespoons extra-virgin olive oil, divided

3 cloves garlic, minced

1 tablespoon fresh thyme or 1 teaspoon dried thyme

½ teaspoon fine sea salt, divided

1 pound flaky, white fish (Pacific halibut, Pacific cod, snapper, tilapia, sole)

Ground black pepper

½ lemon, thinly sliced

*\*Cook times will vary depending on the thickness of the fillet. If your fish is very thin, we recommend prebaking the veggies for 15 minutes prior to adding the fish.*

While you wait for the fish to bake, go put your legs up the wall for a quick rejuvenation trick (see Shalane's Active Recovery Stretches, page 168).

The ingredients in this dish are inspired by Elyse's favorite dinners from her time spent in southern France while working abroad in Switzerland. Baking a light and flaky white fish together with cherry tomatoes, green beans, fresh herbs, and lemons keeps it moist and flavorful.

We all know we should be eating more fish for a healthy hit of nutrients from omega-3 fatty acids to vitamin D, but it can be hard to branch out from chicken and beef. We hope this refreshing one-dish meal will inspire you to explore the sea. **SERVES 4**

1  Preheat the oven to 400°F.

2  In a 9 x 13-inch casserole dish, combine the green beans, tomatoes, olives or capers, 2 tablespoons of the oil, garlic, thyme, and ¼ teaspoon of the salt. Spread out to fill the bottom.

3  Lay the fish on top of the veggies, sprinkle with the remaining ¼ teaspoon salt and a few grinds of pepper, drizzle with the remaining 2 tablespoons of oil, and place the lemon slices on top.

4  Bake for 25 to 30 minutes,\* or until the fish flakes easily with a fork and the green beans are tender but crisp.

**GLUTEN-FREE // DAIRY-FREE**

# TEMPEH RATATOUILLE

*FOR PROTEIN-POWER*

3 tablespoons extra-virgin olive oil

1 yellow onion, chopped

1 teaspoon fine sea salt

2 zucchini (about 1 pound), sliced into half moons

1 eggplant (about 1 pound), cut into 1-inch cubes

6 cloves garlic, roughly chopped

2 teaspoons dried oregano

1 teaspoon dried thyme

1 can (28 ounces) diced tomatoes

1 package (8 ounces) tempeh, cubed, or 1 can (15 ounces) chickpeas (garbanzo beans), rinsed and drained

2 to 3 tablespoons balsamic vinegar

¼ teaspoon ground black pepper

Torn fresh basil leaves (optional)

Ratatouille is a traditional French country dish that provides a healthy hit of veggies. We revamped this dish to suit a runner's needs by adding in protein-packed, mineral-rich tempeh.

Serve as a simple vegan main dish with a crusty baguette. Leftovers make a fun pizza or pasta topping. If you can't find tempeh, feel free to sub in chickpeas. **SERVES 5**

**1** Heat the oil in a large heavy-bottomed pot over medium heat. Add the onion and salt and cook, stirring occasionally, until softened but not brown, about 5 minutes.

**2** Add the zucchini, eggplant, garlic, oregano, and thyme. Cook, stirring occasionally, until the veggies begin to soften, about 8 minutes.

**3** Add the tomatoes and tempeh (or chickpeas) and bring to a simmer. Reduce heat, cover, and simmer for 25 minutes, stirring occasionally.

**4** Turn off the heat and stir in the vinegar and pepper. Taste and season with more salt or vinegar, if needed. Garnish with basil, if desired.

**GLUTEN-FREE // VEGAN**

# SIMPLY ROASTED VEGETABLES

*FOR A HEALTHY HIT*

**2 pounds veggies, peeled and chopped into 1-inch pieces\***

**2 tablespoon extra-virgin olive oil**

**½ teaspoon fine sea salt**

**¼ teaspoon freshly ground black pepper**

*\*Denser root vegetables (beets, parsnips, rutabaga) take longer to cook than veggies like Brussels sprouts and squash, so they should be cut smaller for even cook times.*

**Spice things up:** Try sprinkling the veggies with your favorite spice combos prior to roasting. We love curry powder, cumin, garlic powder, and/or smoked paprika.

For a nutrient boost while training for the Boston Marathon, Shalane kept her fridge stocked with roasted veggies to add to salads, rice bowls, and egg scrambles.

Steamed broccoli gives vegetables a bad reputation—bland and boring. Mix up the vegetable side dish on your table to ensure you're getting a broad range of nutrients. A little roasting love transforms root vegetables, squash, and cruciferous veggies into rock stars.

This recipe works superbly with any combo of hearty veggies that hold up well to high-heat roasting. Try parsnips, beets, Brussels sprouts, rutabaga, carrots, cauliflower, sweet potatoes, and butternut squash. **SERVES 4**

---

**1** Preheat the oven to 425°F. Line a rimmed baking sheet with parchment paper.

**2** Pat the veggies dry and place them on the baking sheet. Toss with the oil, salt, and pepper and spread out.

**3** Roast in the center of the oven, tossing once after 15 minutes, until tender in the center and beginning to brown, 30 to 35 minutes.

**4** Serve warm right out of the oven as a side dish or cool and toss into salads (see DIY Grain Salad, page 95).

**GLUTEN-FREE // VEGAN**

# SUNDAY SWEET POTATOES
### FOR WEEKLY MEAL-PREPPING

**2 large sweet potatoes (about 1½ pounds)**

**2 tablespoons extra-virgin olive oil**

**½ teaspoon garlic powder**

**½ teaspoon fine sea salt**

---

If you're cooking for a family, double this recipe. You'll want to spread the potatoes out on 2 baking sheets, as they need breathing room to caramelize.

Sweet potato skins are packed with nutrients, including potassium and iron, and fiber. Simply give them a good washing and roast with the skin on. Anytime Elyse bakes whole sweet potatoes for recipes like Sweet Potato Waffles (page 82) she saves the skins for Huck, her energetic pup.

Olympic marathoner Amy Cragg's favorite pizza is topped with roasted sweet potatoes, and we've got the recipe (see page 131).

We call these Sunday Sweet Potatoes because we want to encourage you to roast this versatile side dish every Sunday to prep for the week ahead. You'll thank us when you come home from work or school famished and need a nourishing meal pronto.

Sweet potatoes are a runner's best friend—an easy-to-digest complex carb that's loaded with potassium and a broad range of vitamins. We love having leftovers to toss into scrambled eggs, Power Bowls (page 122), and salads (Sweet Potato Salad, page 101). **SERVES 5 AS A SIDE DISH (MAKES 3 CUPS)**

---

**1** Preheat the oven to 425°F. Line a baking sheet with parchment paper. Cut the sweet potatoes into small 1-inch cubes, leaving the skin on (see tip).

**2** Place the sweet potatoes on the baking sheet and toss with the olive oil, garlic powder, and salt. Spread out so that they aren't touching.

**3** Bake for 15 minutes, stir, and return to the oven for 10 to 15 minutes, or until the edges begin to brown.

**4** Leftover roasted sweet potatoes should be refrigerated as soon as they cool to keep them fresh for up to 5 days.

**GLUTEN-FREE // VEGAN**

# ROASTED CAULIFLOWER AND POTATOES

*FOR WHOLE FOOD CARBO-LOADING*

1 pound small red potatoes, cut into bite-size pieces

3 tablespoons extra-virgin olive oil, divided

2 tablespoons minced fresh rosemary or 2 teaspoons dried rosemary

½ teaspoon fine sea salt, divided

¼ teaspoon freshly ground black pepper

1 head cauliflower (about 1½ pounds), rinsed, dried, cut into florets

The Sweet Potato Fries from our first book and this recipe were Shalane's favorite veggie side dishes while training for the NYC Marathon.

Learn to multitask in the kitchen. While you wait for the veggies to roast, prep the rest of dinner and pack your lunch for the next day or blend up a breakfast smoothie. Have you tried our Immune-Boost Smoothie (page 55)?!

This is one of our favorite vegetable side dish combos. The potatoes satisfy our craving for energizing carbs, and the cauliflower adds a healthy hit of antioxidants and inflammation-fighting superpowers.

Don't knock the basic potato. Potatoes are a nutrient-dense whole food high in B vitamins, potassium, and vitamin C. They provide easy-to-digest complex carbs to restore your glycogen levels (and they're easy on the wallet). **SERVES 5**

**1** Preheat the oven to 425°F and line a baking sheet with parchment paper.

**2** Place the potatoes on the baking sheet and toss with 2 tablespoons of the olive oil, the rosemary, ¼ teaspoon of the salt, and the pepper. Roast in the center of the oven for 20 minutes.

**3** Remove from the oven and add the cauliflower to the baking sheet. Drizzle with the remaining olive oil and salt and toss with the potatoes.

**4** Spread vegetables out on the baking sheet and roast in the center of the oven until well browned and slightly charred, about 30 minutes.

**GLUTEN-FREE // VEGAN**

*"For is there any practice less selfish, any labor less alienated, any time less wasted, than preparing something delicious and nourishing for people you love?"*

**–MICHAEL POLLAN**

# COCONUT RICE WITH NORI
## *FOR LONG-LASTING ENERGY*

**2 cups short-grain brown rice**

**2 tablespoons virgin coconut oil**

**3 large toasted nori sheets***

**½ teaspoon sea salt**

**Toasted coconut flakes (optional)**

*\*Buy toasted nori stacked in full-size sheets in resealable packages, not the tiny snack-size foil packs.*

To save time and guarantee perfectly cooked rice, we use an Instant Pot pressure cooker (see "Time-Saving Tools," page 35). Simply place 2 cups of rice and 2½ cups of water in your Instant Pot and use the "manual" button to set to 22 minutes followed by a 10-minute pressure release.

Elyse started adding coconut oil to rice for her toddler, Lily, since healthy fat is essential for brain development in kids. Soon she got Shalane hooked on this combo, too. The toasted nori (seaweed) adds beloved umami flavor and essential trace minerals.

This side dish is so simple, yet so whoa-nelly good, that you'll find it on our tables on a weekly basis. Brown rice, for its wealth of nutrition, should be a staple in every runner's life. **SERVES 6**

**1** Cook the rice according to package directions or rice cooker directions. Crumble the sheets of nori into bite-size pieces.

**2** Fluff the cooked rice with a fork. Stir in the coconut oil, nori, and salt. Keep covered until ready to serve. If you're feeling fancy, garnish with toasted coconut flakes.

**3** We love to serve this rice with grilled fish, and it also makes a great base for creative rice bowls (see Power Bowls, page 122).

**GLUTEN-FREE // VEGAN**

# PURPLE CABBAGE SLAW

*FOR REVIVING ALL SYSTEMS*

**YOGURT DRESSING**

½ cup whole milk yogurt*

3 tablespoons minced shallots

2 tablespoons extra-virgin olive oil

1 tablespoon apple cider vinegar

¾ teaspoon fine sea salt

¼ teaspoon ground black pepper

**SLAW**

5 cups thinly sliced red/purple cabbage (remove core)

½ cup cilantro leaves, chopped (optional)

*Learn why we love putting yogurt in dressings on page 101.*

Red cabbage (looks purple to us!) is a cruciferous star. It's loaded with vitamins, minerals, antioxidants, anti-inflammatory compounds, and fiber. It's also one of the least expensive vegetables, giving you the biggest nutrient bang for your buck.

This yogurt-dressed slaw is a side of beauty. It's flavorful and versatile and stays fresh for days (it even gets better the second day). We served it at a casual backyard dinner party with Slow Cooker Pulled Pork (page 137) and brown rice. Also try it married with Chipotle Black Bean Burgers (page 138), Bonk Burgers (page 139), Sweet Potato Chickpea Cakes (page 141), or Honey Balsamic Grilled Chicken (page 135). **SERVES 5**

**1** In a salad bowl, whisk together the yogurt, shallots, oil, vinegar, salt, and pepper. Add the cabbage and cilantro (if using), and toss to combine.

**2** Refrigerate for at least 1 hour prior to serving. Toss again just before serving. Store leftovers in an airtight container in the fridge for up to 5 days.

**GLUTEN-FREE // VEGETARIAN**

# MISO FAST GREENS
## *FOR A DOSE OF VITAMINS*

**1 tablespoon extra-virgin olive oil**

**1 large bunch kale, collards, chard, or mustard greens, stems removed, chopped***

**2 tablespoons Miso Butter or Miso Honey Butter (page 183)**

**2 cloves garlic, minced**

**⅛ teaspoon red pepper flakes (optional)**

**Sesame seeds (optional garnish)**

*\* If using kale or collards, discard the stems and roughly chop the leaves. Rinse and thoroughly dry the leaves (a salad spinner works great for this). If using Swiss chard, the stems are edible and can be chopped and sautéed first prior to adding the leaves (since they take longer to cook).*

Kale lovers will salivate over this side dish, which combines nutrient-dense greens with nourishing butter. And now that we've taught you that high-quality butter is a health food, you have no excuse not to eat your greens.

Leftover sautéed greens are surprisingly satisfying for breakfast with a side of scrambled eggs or piled on top of Avocado Toast (see page 85). We also love these greens on top of Power Bowls (page 122). **SERVES 3**

---

**1** Heat the oil in a large skillet over medium heat. Add the greens and cook, stirring frequently, until wilted, about 2 to 4 minutes (collards take longer to cook than kale).

**2** Add the Miso Butter, garlic, and red pepper flakes (if using), and sauté for 1 minute. Remove pan from the heat and sprinkle with the sesame seeds (if using).

### *BASIC SAUTÉED GREENS*
When in a pinch, skip the Miso Butter and simply sauté the greens in 2 tablespoons of olive oil. Add minced garlic or garlic powder, salt, and pepper to taste. A squeeze of fresh lemon juice added at the end brightens the flavors.

**GLUTEN-FREE // VEGETARIAN**

# SHALANE'S ACTIVE RECOVERY STRETCHES

While the soup simmers, Shalane sneaks in a few active stretches for recovery. Try these simple exercises in your own kitchen while you cook. ☺

---

## >> LEGS UP THE WALL

Lie on your back with your butt snug against the wall and place your legs straight up the wall so you are in an L-shape. This releases the lower back, stimulates blood flow for recovery, and stretches your hammies. Hang out here for 5 to 10 minutes while practicing deep breathing.

## >> LEG SWINGS

Hold on to the counter with one hand and do 10 forward and backward leg swings on each side to open up your hips and hamstrings.

## >> QUAD STRETCH

Balance on one foot while you grab your other foot from behind with your opposite hand and pull back toward your butt. Keep your glutes activated. Bonus points if you can do this while stirring something on the stovetop.

## >> CALF RAISES

Hang one heel off a step while holding on to the railing and slowly rise up and lower down until your heel is below the step. Do 20 calf raises on each leg to stretch and strengthen the Achilles tendon and calf muscle.

## >> HIP FLEXOR LUNGE

Start in a lunge position with your front knee at 90 degrees. Begin to straighten your back leg, so you feel a stretch along your back thigh. Keep your front knee aligned over your toes. Raise the opposite arm from the lunged leg and reach up high. This should provide a great stretch at the front of your quad and hip flexor. Hold for 15 counts and then switch to the opposite side.

> "I lay out my competition clothes and pack my bag the night before a race so when I wake up in the morning, everything is ready to go. When you get nervous, it's easy to be forgetful!"
>
> **—SHALANE**
> *(READ MORE RACE TIPS ON PAGE 239.)*

# 7|SAUCY

*"I've always taken the philosophy that you have to dream a little in this sport. If you stay in your comfort zone, you're not going to do anything special."*

**—DEENA KASTOR**

# PRESTO PESTO
## FOR DINNER AT THE READY

2 cups tightly packed basil leaves (or arugula)

6-ounce wedge Parmesan, rind removed, quartered

½ cup roasted almonds*

1 clove garlic

½ cup extra-virgin olive oil

¼ cup lemon juice

½ teaspoon fine sea salt

*Mix up your nutz! This pesto is amazing made with almonds, walnuts, cashews, or hazelnuts. Roast your nuts to enhance their flavor (see page 201).

**Nut allergy?** Sub in ½ cup roasted pumpkin seeds for the almonds.

Double this recipe and freeze in small containers (large ice cube trays work great!) for the convenience of easy-to-thaw proportions.

Pesto is so versatile and incredibly nutritious that we keep it stocked in our freezers year-round. It's loaded with raw garlic and herbs, making it both an immune booster and inflammation fighter. Elyse's toddler, Lily, eats it by the spoonful right out of the jar. Shalane relied on this recipe to keep herself healthy through the flu season while training for the 2018 Boston Marathon.

Here's a few of our favorite recipes that put this pesto to work: Pesto Tuna Melt (page 107), Pesto Pasta with Sardines (page 148), Pesto Yogurt Dip (page 175), and Pizza Cali (page 132).

**MAKES 2 CUPS**

**1** In a food processor or high-speed blender, combine the basil (or arugula), Parmesan, nuts, and garlic. Pulse until finely ground. Add the oil, lemon juice, and salt. Process until smooth, scraping down the sides as needed, until fully blended.

**2** Transfer to a widemouthed glass jar and store in the refrigerator for up to 5 days.

**GLUTEN-FREE // VEGETARIAN // VEGAN:** Sub in ½ cup white beans and 1 tablespoon + 1 teaspoon mellow (white) miso paste instead of the Parmesan.

*"If you have the courage to fail, then you have the courage to succeed."*

**–SHALANE**

# PESTO YOGURT DIP
## FOR WHOLESOME SNACKING

½ cup pesto (see Presto Pesto, page 172)

½ cup plain whole milk yogurt

Chopped basil or parsley (optional)

---

Leftover dip is amazing drizzled on top of rice bowls (see Power Bowls, page 122).

If you're as obsessed with making pesto as we are, you'll want to get creative with how you use up every last spoonful. We discovered combining leftover pesto in equal portions with whole milk yogurt transforms it into a luscious dip—a winning dinner party appetizer.

To impress your guests, serve this dip with roasted cauliflower (see Simply Roasted Vegetables for cooking instructions, page 159). **MAKES 1 CUP**

---

In a small serving bowl, combine the pesto and yogurt. Garnish with the fresh herbs (if using). Serve as a dip with tortilla chips, roasted cauliflower, or baby carrots.

**GLUTEN-FREE // VEGETARIAN**

# SMOKY SUMMER SALSA
## FOR KICKING IT UP A NOTCH

**1 pound tomatoes, quartered**

**½ red onion, roughly chopped**

**1 chipotle pepper in adobe sauce***

**Juice of 1 or 2 limes (2 to 3 tablespoons)**

**½ teaspoon fine sea salt**

*\*Canned chipotle peppers can be found on the ethnic food aisle at most grocery stores. We use them in several recipes in this book to add a delicious smoky spice flavor. Freeze leftover chipotle peppers spread out in a quart-size zipper bag to make it easy to break off just the amount needed.*

Once you make homemade salsa, you'll never go back to the store-bought stuff, which is loaded with preservatives and lacks fresh flavor. This restaurant-style salsa can be whirled up in less time than it takes Shalane to run a mile. Simply toss all of the below into a blender or food processor.

Your salsa is only as good as your tomatoes. Save this recipe to make during the summer months. Even better, use backyard or farmers' market tomatoes. **MAKES 3 CUPS**

**1** Place the tomatoes, onion, chipotle pepper, juice of 1 lime, and salt in a food processor or blender and pulse to desired consistency. Taste and add more salt and/or lime juice, if needed.

**2** Divide between two pint-size glass jars (give one to a running buddy!) and chill in the fridge for at least 1 hour prior to serving.

**3** Leftover salsa should be stored in the fridge and will stay fresh for up to 1 week.

**GLUTEN-FREE // VEGAN**

# GARLICKY GUAC

### FOR BODY-LOVING NUTRITION

**1 large or 2 small ripe avocados, pitted**

**½ cup chopped tomatoes**

**2 cloves garlic, minced**

**¼ teaspoon fine sea salt**

**Fresh lime juice, to taste**

---

🕐 As previously mentioned, Shalane's least favorite kitchen work is mincing garlic (unlike Elyse, Shalane really doesn't mind washing dishes!). She highly recommends investing in a quality garlic press, since we use a lot of garlic in this book (see "Time-Saving Tools," page 35).

As you've probably noticed, we're slightly obsessed with avocados. We use them in everything from smoothies to creamy desserts. For athletes, avocados are truly podium-worthy. They are rich in inflammation-fighting nutrients, heart-healthy fats and fiber, powerful antioxidants, and body-loving vitamins and minerals. In fact, avocados are higher in potassium than any other food—adios muscle cramps!

While there are endless ways to savor this creamy fruit, guacamole is the leader of the pack. This versatile condiment transforms simple dinners into memorable meals. We devour it on top of beans and rice with a fried egg for a quick weeknight dinner. And we love to slather guac on burgers, wraps, tacos, tortilla chips, and more. **MAKES 1 CUP**

---

**1** Scoop the avocado into a medium bowl and mash well with a fork.

**2** Stir in the tomato, garlic, salt, and lime juice. Taste and add more salt or lime juice, if needed.

**GLUTEN-FREE // VEGAN**

# GREEN GODDESS TAHINI SAUCE (AND DRESSING)

*FOR FIGHTING INFLAMMATION*

½ cup whole milk yogurt*

½ cup basil leaves

¼ cup parsley leaves

¼ cup tahini (ground sesame seeds)

2 tablespoons lemon juice

1 clove garlic

¼ teaspoon fine sea salt

*Learn why we love yogurt as a sub for mayo on page 101.*

You'll fall in love with this sauce not only for its whoa-nelly flavor, but also for its incredible health benefits. Our unique take on Green Goddess dressing is loaded with fresh basil and parsley, flavorful herbs with anti-inflammatory superpowers. The raw garlic adds a kick and a boost to your immune system. And last but not least, you'll get in a dose of healthy fats from the calcium-rich yogurt and magnesium-rich tahini.

Serve as a dip with crudités or pita chips, spoon it over Power Bowls (page 122) or burgers (page 139), or use as a dressing on your favorite salad. **MAKES 1 CUP**

**1** In a small food processor or high-speed blender, combine the yogurt, basil, parsley, tahini, lemon juice, garlic, and salt. Process until smooth and creamy. If serving as a dip, use as is. If using as a sauce or dressing, add a little water to thin it to your desired consistency.

**2** This sauce can be made without an appliance by finely chopping the herbs and garlic and stirring all of the ingredients together.

**3** Stays fresh for up to 1 week in the fridge.

**GLUTEN-FREE // VEGETARIAN // VEGAN:** Create a dairy-free variation made with cashews instead of yogurt. Boil ½ cup water, add ¼ cup cashews, cover, remove from heat, and soak for 30 minutes (do not discard water). Blend the cashews and the soaking water with the above ingredients.

*"Since adding more fat and whole foods into my diet, my racing weight now comes naturally—without counting calories. Hallelujah!!!!"*

**—SHALANE**

# CREAMY GINGER CASHEW SAUCE (AND DRESSING)

*FOR FAT FLAVOR*

1 cup raw cashews

¼ cup lemon juice

2 cloves garlic

2 tablespoons grated ginger

1 tablespoon extra-virgin olive oil

1 tablespoon + 1 teaspoon soy sauce

Sauces are the way to transform a simple dish into a memorable meal that will leave you feeling satisfied. Our vegan Creamy Ginger Cashew Sauce provides a healthy dose of fats that help your body absorb fat-soluble vitamins.

This versatile sauce is happy on anything. Try it drizzled on top of steaming bowls of rice with sautéed veggies. See Power Bowls (page 122) for inspiration. Use it as a salad dressing or serve as a dip with roasted cauliflower or carrots and celery sticks. **MAKES 1½ CUPS**

---

**1** Boil ¾ cup water, add the cashews, cover, remove from heat, and soak for 30 minutes (do not discard water). Place the cashews, the soaking water, lemon juice, garlic, ginger, oil, and soy sauce in a high-speed blender or food processor and blend until completely smooth.

**2** To transform into a salad dressing, thin with a tablespoon or two of water.

**3** Store in an airtight container in the fridge for up to 5 days. This sauce also freezes well.

### TEX-MEX VARIATION

Substitute 1 tablespoon of chili powder for the fresh ginger. Use this variation to create a vegan dressing for our Southwest Salad (page 98).

**GLUTEN-FREE // VEGAN**

# TURMERIC COCONUT CURRY SAUCE
## FOR REVIVING DINNER (AND YOURSELF)

1 tablespoon extra-virgin olive oil or coconut oil

1 yellow onion, chopped

½ teaspoon fine sea salt

3 cloves garlic, chopped

1 tablespoon curry powder

1 teaspoon ground turmeric

¼ teaspoon cayenne

1 can (13.5 ounces) coconut milk

Store sauce in a glass jar in the fridge for up to 1 week. Freeze leftover sauce in individual portions (we recommend using freezer-safe half-pint glass jars) and keep stocked in your freezer to help you pull off last-minute meals.

Homemade sauces are your new secret weapon. Sauces add richness, flavor, and depth to simple dishes, ensuring that you feel satiated at the end of a meal. The healthy fats in sauces are nourishing, restorative, and help with nutrient absorption. Add in spices and you've got inflammation-fighting powers.

Drizzle this spicy coconut curry sauce on the most basic weeknight meals to transform them into magic. We love it on top of Power Bowls (page 122) with Crispy Tempeh (page 143). Recipe tester Brittany Williams also highly recommends it slathered on baked fish. **MAKES 2½ CUPS**

**1** Heat the oil in a medium saucepan over medium-high heat. Add the onion and salt and cook, stirring occasionally, until the onions are soft but not brown, about 5 minutes. Add the garlic, curry powder, turmeric, and cayenne and cook, stirring frequently, for 1 minute (be careful not to burn the spices).

**2** Stir in the coconut milk and bring to a boil. Reduce the heat to low and simmer, uncovered, stirring occasionally, until the sauce thickens and the flavors meld, about 10 minutes.

**3** Use an immersion (stick) blender to blend the sauce until smooth. Alternatively, transfer the sauce to a blender and process until smooth. To save time, this sauce can also be left chunky.

**4** To serve, fill a bowl with cooked brown rice or quinoa, add your favorite sautéed or roasted veggies and protein (beans, tempeh, chicken, steak, fried egg, etc.), and spoon the sauce generously over top.

**GLUTEN-FREE // VEGAN**

# BASIC PIZZA SAUCE
*FOR PIZZA AT THE READY*

1 28-ounce can crushed tomatoes (use a high-quality brand like Muir Glen)

2 tablespoons extra-virgin olive oil

2 cloves garlic, minced

½ teaspoon fine sea salt

Skip buying expensive, sugary jars of pizza sauce. This simple sauce lets the other ingredients on your pizza shine and there's no need to simmer it, as it will cook right on the pizza.

This recipe makes enough sauce for three 12-inch pizzas. Freeze leftovers for future pizza-making shenanigans. You can also use this as a base for making a quick Marinara or Bolognese Sauce (see below). **MAKES 3 CUPS**

1 In a large glass container with a lid, combine the tomatoes, olive oil, garlic, and salt. That's it. You're done. If using this sauce on pizza, there's no need to simmer it.

2 Use about 1 cup of sauce per 12-inch pizza and spread evenly over the dough (see Amy's Recovery Pizza on page 131 for further pizza instructions).

3 Store in the fridge for up to 5 days or divide between 1-cup size freezer-safe containers and freeze for up to 3 months.

### BASIC MARINARA SAUCE (MAKES 2 CUPS)
Combine the above ingredients in a large saucepan and bring to a boil. Reduce the heat to low and simmer uncovered for 30 minutes, or until the sauce thickens. Season to taste. Better yet, simmer this sauce with Turkey Trot Meatballs (page 147).

### BASIC BOLOGNESE SAUCE
In a large saucepan, brown 1 pound of ground meat in a little oil. Add the sauce ingredients above and bring to a boil. Reduce the heat to low and simmer uncovered for 30 minutes, or until the sauce thickens. Season to taste. Or try our veggie-loaded Marathon Bolognese recipe on page 144.

**GLUTEN-FREE // VEGAN**

# MISO BUTTER
### FOR AN UMAMI FLAVOR BOOST

½ stick (4 tablespoons)
unsalted butter

2 tablespoons miso paste

Keep this simple compound butter on hand to add instant umami flavor to cooked veggies (try it on steamed broccoli, sautéed greens, grilled corn, baked potatoes, and more). We especially love it on baked salmon (see Miso Butter Salmon, page 155), and we're addicted to Miso Fast Greens (page 167). When Shalane has a serious salt craving, she adores it straight up smeared on toast.

Miso is a fermented food, which makes it rich in probiotics and easy to digest. Look for a mild miso paste, usually called "white" or "mellow." It can be found at health food grocery stores or online. Our favorite brand is Miso Master. **MAKES ¼ CUP**

---

**1** Leave your butter at room temperature until softened. In a small bowl, use a fork to combine the butter and miso until well blended.

**2** Leftover Miso Butter will keep in the fridge in a sealed container for up to 2 weeks.

### MISO HONEY BUTTER
Add 1 tablespoon honey to the above. Use it on Miso Butter Salmon (page 155).

**GLUTEN-FREE // VEGETARIAN**

# LEMON MISO DRESSING
## FOR CRAVE-WORTHY SALADS

½ cup extra-virgin olive oil

⅓ cup lemon juice

2 or 3 cloves garlic, minced

2 teaspoons miso paste (preferably mellow white)

½ teaspoon fine sea salt

¼ teaspoon ground black pepper

 For a sweet variation, add a tablespoon of honey to the ingredients. Best dressing ever.

This is our signature dressing from the first cookbook, so we had to bring it back! And just for you we've added an orange-ginger variation. Try either one of these super-duper miso dressings on your fave hearty grain salads.

The Lemon Miso Dressing pairs perfectly with Veggie Lovers Pasta Salad (page 105) and the Orange Miso variation is heavenly in the Kale and Edamame Salad (page 96). **MAKES ABOUT 1 CUP**

Combine the oil, lemon juice, garlic, miso, salt, and pepper in a glass jar with a lid. Use a fork to stir in the miso, then seal, and shake vigorously to emulsify.

**GLUTEN-FREE // VEGAN**

# ORANGE MISO DRESSING
## FOR MIXING UP THE MAGIC

⅓ cup extra-virgin olive oil

⅓ cup orange juice (preferably fresh-squeezed)

¼ cup apple cider vinegar

1 tablespoon miso paste (preferably mellow white)

1 teaspoon grated fresh ginger (optional)

½ teaspoon fine sea salt

¼ teaspoon ground black pepper

Combine the oil, orange juice, vinegar, miso, ginger (if using), salt, and pepper in a glass jar with a lid. Use a fork to stir in the miso, then seal, and shake vigorously to emulsify.

**GLUTEN-FREE // VEGAN**

Both dressings will keep in the fridge for up to 1 week. If the oil solidifies, briefly microwave on low until melted.

*Elyse, 7-months' pregnant, with daughter, Lily, during the summer cookbook photoshoot at Brasada Ranch.*

# APPLE CIDER VINAIGRETTE
## FOR DIGESTIVE RESTORATION

½ cup extra-virgin olive oil

⅓ cup apple cider vinegar

2 tablespoons Dijon mustard

2 tablespoons minced shallot or 1 or 2 cloves garlic, minced

---

Make it creamy. Add a tablespoon of tahini to the ingredients.

Apple cider vinegar is our go-to vinegar since it's inexpensive and awesome for digestion. It's also high in essential minerals, including potassium and magnesium, and its acidic nature helps kill off bad bacteria in the body, making it a natural immune booster.

Look for raw apple cider vinegar with a cloudiness, which means it's full of good probiotics. Our favorite brand is Bragg Organic Raw and Unfiltered.

We keep a stash of this dressing in our fridge at all times since it pairs great with just about any salad (see DIY Grain Salad, page 95). **MAKES 1 CUP**

---

**1** Combine the oil, vinegar, mustard, and shallot or garlic in a glass jar with a lid. Shake vigorously until emulsified.

**2** This basic vinaigrette pairs happily with any refreshing salad.

**3** This dressing will keep in the fridge for up to 1 week. If the oil solidifies, briefly microwave on low until melted.

**GLUTEN-FREE // VEGAN**

# QUICK-PICKLE RED ONIONS

## *FOR DRESSING UP BURGERS AND BOWLS*

½ cup apple cider vinegar

2 tablespoons honey

2 teaspoons fennel seeds

1 teaspoon fine sea salt

1 red onion, thinly sliced

---

Add a simple dinner salad to your meal in minutes. Salad greens topped with these onions, pumpkin seeds or walnuts, and a drizzle of olive oil does the trick.

In a pickle? Escape the madness with these tangy, sweet, and spicy pickled red onions. Quick-pickled fresh veggies take 5 minutes tops to prepare and will last for weeks in your fridge. They hit on so many different flavor notes to satisfy your taste buds.

We make our pickled onions with apple cider vinegar for its host of health benefits—it stimulates digestion, boosts immunity, detoxifies, and is rich in enzymes, probiotics, potassium, and magnesium.

You can use this as a base for pickling any assortment of leftover veggies—get creative with radishes, cucumbers, green beans, roasted beets, and/or carrots. **MAKES 1 PINT**

---

**1** Stir together the vinegar, honey, fennel seeds, and salt in a pint-size glass jar. Add the onions and press down until they are fully submerged in the liquid.

**2** Seal with the lid, leave out at room temperature for 1 hour, and then refrigerate until ready to use.

**3** This quick pickle is ready to serve after just a few hours but will be even better the next day.

**4** Stays fresh in the fridge for up to 3 weeks.

**GLUTEN-FREE // VEGETARIAN // DAIRY-FREE**

# 8 | POWER SNACKS (SAVORY)

*"Run for those who cannot run. Appreciate your health, your body, and your ability to push yourself."*

**—SHALANE**

# SAVORY PRETZEL GRANOLA
## *FOR SALTY SNACKING SATISFACTION*

3 cups pretzels (twists)

2 cups nuts (almonds and cashews)

1 cup old-fashioned rolled oats

½ cup sunflower seeds

2 teaspoons mustard powder

1 teaspoon garlic or onion powder

½ teaspoon fine sea salt

¼ teaspoon cayenne (optional)

2 egg whites (save the yolks for breakfast!)

2 tablespoons extra-virgin olive oil

2 tablespoons honey

---

Divide among snack-size zipper bags so that you can grab one in the morning on your way out the door.

Elyse developed this recipe for a recent *Runner's World* holiday issue, and it turned out so addictively good that Shalane requested we sneak it into the book.

Fuel your snack-attack needs with a crunchy, salty treat you can feel good about devouring. This unique savory granola is high in protein and healthy fats. **MAKES 7 CUPS**

---

**1** Preheat the oven to 275°F and line a rimmed baking sheet with parchment paper.

**2** In a large mixing bowl, combine the pretzels, nuts, oats, seeds, mustard powder, garlic or onion powder, salt, and cayenne (if using). In a small bowl, whisk together the egg whites, olive oil, and honey. Add to the dry ingredients and toss to combine.

**3** Spread out on the baking sheet. Bake for 35 to 40 minutes, stirring after 20 minutes, until lightly browned. Cool completely.

**4** Store in a glass canister in your pantry for up to 2 weeks.

**VEGETARIAN** // **GLUTEN-FREE:** Use certified gluten-free oats and pretzels.

# MISO KALE CHIPS

## FOR NEXT-LEVEL CHIPS

1 large bunch of kale (curly variety), stems removed

½ cup raw cashews

2 tablespoons olive oil

2 teaspoons white or mellow miso

½ teaspoon garlic powder

½ teaspoon smoked paprika, optional

*\*If you don't have 2 baking sheets, you'll need to cook them in 2 batches. The kale will not get crispy if over-crowded. Don't be sur-prised—they shrink a lot.*

These next-level kale chips take a little love to prepare, but are worth the effort. They're coated in an addicting savory cashew paste, which makes them extra crispy. So good you'll probably want to hide them from hungry housemates and husbands. Leverage these chips to transform kale haters into lovers.

**SERVES 4**

---

**1** Preheat the oven to 300°F and line 2 rimmed baking sheets\* with parchment paper. Wash and dry the kale leaves thoroughly and tear into pieces.

**2** In a small food processor, combine the cashews, olive oil, miso, garlic, and paprika and pulse until finely ground (it will form a paste).

**3** In a large bowl, toss the kale with the miso mixture and use your hands to work it evenly into the crevices of the leaves.

**4** Spread the kale out on the baking sheets. Bake in the center of the oven for 10 minutes, rotate the pan and return to the oven for another 7 to 10 minutes, or until crispy. Watch carefully as kale chips are easy to burn (we know because we destroyed a couple batches during recipe testing).

**5** Allow to cool, then serve. Chow down—kale chips lose their crispiness by the next day (but are still good!).

**GLUTEN-FREE // VEGAN**

*Shalane hammering through 400-meter repeats with Nike Bowerman teammate Emily Infeld, at training camp in St. Moritz, Switzerland.*

# SWEET POTATO HUMMUS
## FOR HAPPY-HEALTHY SNACKING

1 can (15 ounces) chickpeas (garbanzo beans), rinsed and drained

½ cup mashed cooked sweet potato (yams; see page 141 for cooking instructions)

¼ cup fresh lemon juice

¼ cup extra-virgin olive oil

3 tablespoons water

2 tablespoons tahini

1 clove garlic

½ teaspoon fine sea salt

½ teaspoon smoked paprika*

¼ teaspoon ground cinnamon

¼ teaspoon cayenne (optional—to add a kick)

*Smoked paprika is a versatile spice that you'll want to put on everything once you try it. If you can't track it down, sub in regular paprika or ground cumin.

Tahini is made from ground sesame seeds and is high in minerals. We love it in salad dressings (page 178) and granola bars (page 229). But if you don't want to add another ingredient to your shopping list, you can sub in almond butter or an extra tablespoon of olive oil.

Transform leftover hummus into a luscious sauce for rice bowls by thinning it with a little broth or water and warming briefly in the microwave.

Since you loved the Don't Get Beet Hummus in our first cookbook, we were inspired to create another unique hummus combo. Hummus is an ideal base for sneaking more veggies into your life. This time we added sweet potatoes to satisfy both sweet and savory snack cravings.

Devour this satisfying spread anytime of the day: Smear it on toast for breakfast, serve in a wrap with veggies for a protein-packed vegetarian lunch (see Mediterranean Hummus Wrap, page 108), dollop on top of burgers or rice bowls for a quick dinner, serve as a crowd-pleasing appetizer with pita or tortilla chips, or pack in a small glass jar with carrot and celery sticks.

**MAKES 2 CUPS**

1  In a food processor or high-speed blender, combine the garbanzo beans, sweet potato, lemon juice, oil, water, tahini, garlic, salt, paprika, cinnamon, and cayenne (if using). Process on high until smooth, stopping as needed to scrape down the sides and underneath the blade with a rubber spatula.

2  Transfer to a small serving bowl and garnish with a drizzle of olive oil and a sprinkle of paprika.

3  Store leftovers in the fridge for up to 5 days.

**GLUTEN-FREE // VEGAN**

# CRISPY CHICKPEAS
## FOR GUILT-FREE SNACKING

1 can (15 ounces) chickpeas (garbanzo beans), rinsed and drained

2 tablespoons extra-virgin olive oil

½ teaspoon smoked paprika

½ teaspoon garlic powder

½ teaspoon fine sea salt

⅛ teaspoon cayenne (optional)

The next time you're feeling an urge to devour a bag of chips, try making this pop-able, addicting snack. These chickpeas are simply seasoned and roasted until crispy. They're great on their own or on top of salads.

Chickpeas are high in protein, fiber, vitamins, and minerals. For vegetarians, they add essential B vitamins. Elyse devoured this snack while pregnant, since chickpeas are especially high in folate. **MAKES 1 CUP**

---

**1** Preheat the oven to 400°F. Line a rimmed baking sheet with parchment paper. Pour chickpeas onto a clean kitchen towel and thoroughly pat dry.

**2** Place chickpeas on the baking sheet and toss with the oil, smoked paprika, garlic powder, salt, and cayenne (if using). Spread out in a single layer.

**3** Bake for 20 minutes, stir, and return to the oven for 10 minutes, or until extra crispy. Allow the chickpeas to cool completely prior to serving.

**GLUTEN-FREE // VEGAN**

# SMOKED SALMON SPREAD
## FOR A BRAIN-BOOSTING APPETIZER

8 ounces cream cheese, softened

6 ounces smoked salmon, chopped

⅓ cup plain whole milk yogurt

Zest of 1 lemon

2 tablespoons lemon juice

¼ teaspoon fine sea salt

Ground black pepper, to taste

Here's an easy-peasy-cheesy spread to whip together when you want to impress your guests. We love that this crowd-pleaser can be served any time of day. For brunch, serve this omega-3 rich spread on toasted bagels or stuffed inside omelets. For dinner, serve it as an appetizer with crostini or use it as a topping on baked sweet potatoes or Wild Rice Pancakes (page 81).

We prefer to use wild, hot smoked salmon (which is fully cooked) for its texture, but traditional raw smoked salmon can also be used. **MAKES 1½ CUPS**

**1** In a medium bowl, use a fork to blend the cream cheese, salmon, yogurt, lemon zest, lemon juice, salt, and pepper. Alternatively, the ingredients can be blended quickly with a food processor.

**2** Spoon into a serving dish. Cover and chill in the fridge until ready to serve.

**GLUTEN-FREE**

*Shalane cooking with her coach's daughter, Makenna Schumacher, and the Jesuit High School XC team.*

# NORI POPCORN
## *FOR SALTY SNACKING SATISFACTION*

**5 tablespoons virgin coconut oil, divided**

**½ cup popcorn kernels**

**2 large sheets toasted nori (seaweed)***

**½ to 1 teaspoon fine sea salt**

*\*You can find large sheets of nori (avoid the tiny snack packs) in most natural foods grocery stores or online. Our favorite brand is Emerald Cove. Be sure to get the toasted version for optimal flavor.*

Warning: Don't make this recipe unless you have friends to share it with. This salty, wholesome snack is seriously addicting. We could probably devour the entire bowl in one sitting. That's okay by us, since it's drizzled with nourishing coconut oil instead of artificially flavored butter. And it's topped with seaweed—that counts as eating something green!

Once you pop your own kernels, you'll never go back to the microwave bags. There's something magical about popping it the good old-fashioned way. Plus it's really, truly easy. All you need is a large pan with a tight-fitting lid. **SERVES 4**

---

**1**  Melt 3 tablespoons of the oil in a large pan with a lid over high heat. Once hot, add the kernels and cover with the lid. When the popping really gets going, turn the heat down to medium and give the pan a little shake.

**2**  When the popping slows to just one kernel at a time, remove the pan from heat but keep covered for another minute until the popping stops.

**3**  Transfer the popcorn to a large bowl. Melt remaining 2 tablespoons of oil, drizzle over the top, and toss to coat. Ball up the nori sheets in your hands and crumble over top. Add salt to taste and stir to combine.

**4**  Leftover popcorn will stay fresh in an airtight container for up to 3 days.

### *POP IT UP*
Experiment with creating your own flavor combos! Try cinnamon and coconut sugar or Parmesan and black pepper, or spice it up a notch with smoked paprika, turmeric, and garlic powder.

**GLUTEN-FREE // VEGAN**

*"Good things come to those who sweat."*

**–UNKNOWN**
*(FAVORITE QUOTE WE HEARD
WHILE ON OUR BOOK TOUR)*

# MAPLE TURMERIC NUTS

**FOR A PODIUM-WORTHY RECOVERY SNACK**

3½ cups (16 ounces) whole, raw nuts (cashews, hazelnuts, almonds)

2 tablespoons maple syrup

2 tablespoons virgin coconut oil, melted (or olive oil)

1 teaspoon ground turmeric

½ teaspoon ground cinnamon

½ teaspoon fine sea salt

⅛ teaspoon cayenne (optional)

Crazy for a healthier snack option? Go nutz! Nuts are rich in heart-healthy monounsaturated fatty acids and essential minerals like magnesium and zinc. Magnesium is vital for healthy bones and relaxed muscles. Muscle cramps and tightness can be a sign of not having enough magnesium in your diet—a common deficiency among runners.

As an added bonus, this snack has inflammation-fighting superpowers from the incredible combo of cinnamon and turmeric. Serve as an easy appetizer when fast friends make a surprise visit. **MAKES 3½ CUPS**

**1** Preheat the oven to 350°F. Line a rimmed baking sheet with parchment paper.

**2** In a large bowl, combine the nuts, maple syrup, and oil. Sprinkle the turmeric, cinnamon, salt, and cayenne (if using), over top and toss to coat evenly.

**3** Spread the nuts on the baking sheet and roast in the center of the oven for 8 to 12 minutes, stirring every 4 minutes, until the nuts turn slightly darker.

**4** Allow to cool completely and then store in a glass jar.

**GLUTEN-FREE // VEGAN**

# BASIC DRY ROASTED NUTS

## FOR VERSATILITY

*Cook times vary. Almonds take longer to roast than walnuts.*

Roasting nuts enhances their flavor and digestibility. Nuts for salads, pesto, nut butter, muesli, and more can be simply dry roasted.

---

**1** Preheat the oven to 350°F. Spread nuts out in a single layer on a rimmed baking sheet.

**2** Bake in the center of the oven for 8 to 15* minutes, stirring every 4 minutes or until toasty and fragrant.

**3** Set a timer. Nuts are easy to forget about and can burn quickly (been there, done that!).

**GLUTEN-FREE // VEGAN**

---

## BEST BEDTIME SNACKS

The following foods are high in essential minerals for inducing sleep, including body-relaxing calcium and magnesium. These snacks provide healthy fats to keep you satisfied, so you don't wake up hungry in the middle of the night. (If you *are* waking up with hunger pains in the middle of the night, it's a sign you aren't fueling enough throughout the day.) See more sleep tips on page 150.

>> Whole milk yogurt topped with Honey Cardamom Granola *(page 64)*

>> Strawberry-Rhubarb Chia Parfait *(page 217)*

>> Banana with almond butter or Chai Cashew Butter *(page 222)*

>> Nori Popcorn *(page 198)* or Savory Pretzel Granola *(page 191)*

>> Herbal tea and Ginger Molasses Cookies *(page 208)*

>> Beet Blueberry Molasses Superhero Muffins *(page 63)* or Molasses Granola Bars *(page 229)*

>> Nuts and dried fruit *(see Maple Turmeric Nuts, page 200)*

>> Cheese and apple slices

# 9 | POWER SNACKS (SWEET)

*"Winning doesn't always mean getting first place. It means getting the best out of yourself."*

**—MEB KEFLEZIGHI**

# LEMON HAZELNUT COOKIES

**FOR GLUTEN-FREE COOKIE BLISS**

2½ cups hazelnut meal*

¼ teaspoon baking soda

⅛ teaspoon fine sea salt

¼ cup honey

2 tablespoons virgin coconut oil, melted

1 tablespoon lemon zest (about 1 lemon)

1 tablespoon lemon juice

*Can't find hazelnut meal (aka hazelnut flour)? Make your own by pulsing whole hazelnuts in a food processor or high-speed blender until finely ground (be careful not to over-process or you'll end up with nut butter). Or feel free to sub in almond meal. Since almonds have a lower fat content, add an additional tablespoon of coconut oil.

Honey is a stellar replacement for refined sugar in baked goods, dressings, and sauces. It's an easily absorbable, natural source of glycogen, making it an ideal running fuel. If you can get raw local honey, it's worth the splurge.

This is our new go-to party cookie, since they're a crowd pleaser with both kids and adults. We love that they're free of refined flour and refined sugar and rich in healthy fats. With just four main ingredients, they're a cinch when you're in a pinch.

We're hazelnut lovers since our great state of Oregon grows 99 percent of the US hazelnut crop, but feel free to sub in almond meal (see note). **MAKES 18 SMALL COOKIES**

**1**  Preheat the oven to 350°F and line a rimmed baking sheet with parchment paper.

**2**  In a medium bowl, combine the hazelnut meal, baking soda, and salt. Stir in the honey, melted coconut oil, lemon zest, and lemon juice. The batter will seem dry at first but just keep stirring.

**3**  Roll the batter into tablespoon-size balls. Space on the prepared baking sheet and flatten slightly into a cookie shape.

**4**  Bake for 8 to 10 minutes or until golden brown underneath (use a spatula to sneak a peek). The cookies will be soft and fragile until they cool. Cool completely prior to transferring to a plate.

**GLUTEN-FREE // VEGETARIAN // DAIRY-FREE**

*"They are GREAT as leftovers. Some of the best cookies that I've made that last. They taste the same and have the same texture days later. It's awesome."*

**–GWEN JORGENSEN,** *RECIPE TESTER,*
*2016 OLYMPIC TRIATHLON GOLD MEDALIST*

# OATMEAL CHOCOLATE CHIP COOKIES

## FOR COZY LAZY DAYS

2 cups old-fashioned rolled oats

1½ cups whole-wheat pastry flour*

1 cup chocolate chips

1½ teaspoons baking powder

1 teaspoon baking soda

1 teaspoon fine sea salt

2 sticks unsalted butter, slightly melted

1 cup coconut sugar (or white sugar)

2 eggs

2 teaspoons vanilla

*If you don't have pastry flour, sub in all-purpose whole-wheat flour. The cookies will be more cakey, but still delicious.

Form leftover dough into a 2-inch-wide log. Wrap the log in parchment paper, seal in a gallon-size zipper bag, and store in the freezer for up to 3 months. Remove from the freezer 1 hour prior to baking and use a sharp knife to slice into cookies.

Homemade cookies are the ultimate way to uplift your home and family on a dreary winter day. Here in Oregon we have a lot of days like that. This was one of the first recipes Shalane requested for our second book: a healthier chocolate chip cookie that didn't require an electric mixer.

Baking with whole-grain flour can be tricky. The secret is to not skimp on the butter (Remember, butter is good for you! See page 26). These cookies are best enjoyed warm, right out of the oven. Since this recipe makes a lot, you can freeze half the dough for fresh baked cookies in a pinch (see Time-Saver tip).

**MAKES 24 COOKIES**

**1** Preheat the oven to 350°F and line a baking sheet with parchment paper.

**2** In a large mixing bowl, combine the oats, flour, chocolate chips, baking powder, baking soda, and salt.

**3** In a separate bowl, whisk together the butter, sugar, eggs, and vanilla until well blended.

**4** Add the wet ingredients to the dry and mix until combined (use your muscles as the dough will be thick).

**5** Roll dough into golf ball-sizes, space 1-inch apart on the prepared baking sheet, and flatten slightly.

**6** Bake in the center of the oven for 10 to 12 minutes, or until golden. Use a spatula to transfer the cookies to a baking rack to cool.

**VEGETARIAN**

# GINGER MOLASSES COOKIES

*FOR SWEET DIGESTION*

2 cups whole-wheat pastry flour

½ cup coconut sugar (or white sugar)

1 teaspoon ground cinnamon

1 teaspoon baking soda

¼ teaspoon fine sea salt

1 stick (8 tablespoons) unsalted butter, melted on low in microwave

⅓ cup blackstrap molasses

1 tablespoon grated fresh ginger or 2 teaspoons ground ginger

1 egg

Bake one batch of these and they'll become your new favorite holiday cookie. The enticing combo of molasses and ginger is sweetly satisfying without the sugar overload in store-bought cookies. Blackstrap molasses is crazy high in iron, a key nutrient for performance. Soothing ginger stimulates digestion and helps relieve gas (every runner wants that!).

Don't fear baking with a stick of butter. Buy high-quality organic or grass-fed butter and you're doing your body good. Butter is rich in essential nutrients, and the short and medium-chain fatty acids provide quick energy. **MAKES 24 SMALL COOKIES**

**1** In a large mixing bowl, combine the flour, sugar, cinnamon, baking soda, and salt.

**2** In a separate bowl, whisk the melted butter, molasses, ginger, and egg until blended. Add the wet ingredients to the dry and mix until combined (use your hands to fully incorporate).

**3** Cover the bowl and chill the batter in the fridge for 1 hour (or longer).

**4** Preheat the oven to 350°F and line 2 baking sheets with parchment paper.

**5** Use your hands to roll the dough into tablespoon-size balls and space 2 inches apart on the prepared baking sheets (cookies will flatten out as they bake).

**6** Bake in the center of the oven for 10 to 12 minutes, or until the bottoms of the cookies start to brown.

**7** Use a spatula to transfer the cookies to a cooling rack. Store in an airtight container for up to 5 days.

**VEGETARIAN // GLUTEN-FREE:** Sub in 2 cups of almond meal for the flour and cut the butter in half to 4 tablespoons (since almond meal has a higher moisture and fat content).

# AVOCADO LIME TARTS

*FOR DECADENT NOURISHMENT*

## CRUST

½ cup old-fashioned rolled oats (gluten-free if sensitive)

1 cup dates, pitted

¼ cup sesame seeds

2 tablespoons virgin coconut oil, melted

Pinch of salt

## FILLING

1 large or 2 small ripe avocados

⅓ cup lime juice (about 3 limes)

¼ cup maple syrup

3 tablespoons virgin coconut oil, melted

½ teaspoon vanilla

⅛ teaspoon fine sea salt

Who knew such a decadent dessert could be so nourishing?! Cookbook assistant and nutritionist Natalie Bickford loves key lime pie, but not the sugar overload, so she developed this anti-oxidant-rich, dairy-free, whole-food version.

Avocado makes these tarts super smooth and creamy and gives you a healthy dose of good fats, fiber, B vitamins, and potassium. **MAKES 8**

**1** Line a standard muffin tin with 8 paper muffin cups.

**2** To make the crust: Pulse the oats and dates in a food processor or high-speed blender until finely ground. Add the sesame seeds, coconut oil, and salt. Process until well combined.

**3** Divide the oat crust evenly among the muffin cups and use your fingers to firmly press down to fill the bottoms.

**4** To make the filling: Wipe out the blender or food processor and add the avocado, lime juice, syrup, oil, vanilla, and salt. Blend until smooth, scraping down the sides as needed. Divide the filling evenly and pour on top of each crust. Place in the freezer for at least 1 hour to set.

**5** Transfer to an airtight container and store in the freezer until ready to serve. Take out from the freezer 15 minutes prior to serving.

**GLUTEN-FREE // VEGAN**

# CHOCOLATE PEANUT BUTTER CUPS

**FOR LEGIT CHOCOLATE CRAVINGS**

### CHOCOLATE

⅓ cup virgin coconut oil

¼ cup unsweetened cocoa powder

3 tablespoons maple syrup

### PEANUT BUTTER FILLING

2 tablespoons virgin coconut oil

½ cup peanut butter (made from 100 percent peanuts)

1 tablespoon maple syrup

¼ teaspoon vanilla

⅛ teaspoon fine sea salt

---

If you don't have a mini muffin pan, you can make 6 large peanut butter cups instead. Fill with double the amounts for the chocolate layers and peanut butter layer.

Cookbook assistant Natalie Bickford created this recipe especially for our young fans who have a fondness for Reese's Peanut Butter Cups. She replaced the refined sugars, processed oils, and other additives in her favorite candy with antioxidant-rich whole foods and healthy fats to re-create this classic candy.

Makenna, a high school 2-mile state champ and Shalane's coach's daughter, helped Shalane test many of the recipes in this book, and this was one of her top picks. Shalane's feedback via email simply stated, "TO DIE FOR!!!!!!!" Nuff said. Make 'em tonight! **MAKES 12 MINI CUPS**

---

**1**  Line a mini muffin pan with 12 mini paper muffin cups.

**2**  To make the chocolate: In a small bowl, microwave the coconut oil for 30 seconds, or just until melted. Stir in the cocoa powder and maple syrup.

**3**  Place 1 teaspoon of the chocolate in each muffin cup to fill the bottom. Place the muffin tin in the freezer until the chocolate solidifies, about 5 minutes.

**4**  To make the peanut butter filling: In a small bowl, microwave the coconut oil for 30 seconds, or just until melted. Use a fork to stir in the peanut butter, maple syrup, vanilla, and salt.

**5**  Spoon about a tablespoon of peanut butter filling on top of the chocolate. Then spoon another teaspoon of chocolate on top of the peanut butter filling to fill the cups (if the chocolate begins to harden, microwave it for 10 seconds). Place peanut butter cups in the freezer until solid, about 30 minutes.

**6**  Store in an airtight container in the fridge or freezer. Remove from the freezer 15 minutes prior to serving.

**GLUTEN-FREE // VEGAN**

# CHOCOLATE-MATCHA ENERGY BALLS

*FOR DIGGING DEEP*

### FILLING

½ cup shredded coconut

½ cup dates (Deglet Noor variety)

¾ cup raw pumpkin seeds

2 tablespoons virgin coconut oil

1 tablespoon matcha green tea powder

¼ teaspoon fine sea salt

### DARK CHOCOLATE COATING

2 tablespoons virgin coconut oil

3 tablespoons maple syrup

3 tablespoons unsweetened cocoa powder

Elyse kept a stash of these two-bite, energizing dark chocolate balls in her freezer to grab whenever she needed an energy boost while writing this cookbook. This no-bake dessert is high in antioxidants and minerals from the uplifting combo of green tea, cocoa powder, and pumpkin seeds.

The chocolate coating melts easily, so store in the fridge or freezer. Stashing sweet treats in the freezer is a great way to avoid the temptation to polish off the entire batch in one sitting. Take out 15 minutes prior to devouring.

If you don't have matcha green tea powder, feel free to sub in more cocoa powder or cinnamon. **MAKES 14 BALLS**

---

**1** Line a rimmed baking sheet with parchment paper.

**2** To make the filling: In a food processor or high-speed blender, combine the coconut, dates, seeds, coconut oil, matcha, and salt. Pulse or blend on high, stopping as needed to scrape underneath the blade, until smooth.

**3** Use a tablespoon to scoop a small amount into your hands and roll into a bite-size ball. Continue with the rest of the mixture. Place the balls on the baking sheet and pop in the freezer to chill for 15 minutes.

**4** To make the coating: In a small microwaveable bowl, microwave the coconut oil for 30 seconds, or just until melted. Stir in the maple syrup and cocoa powder.

**5** Drop one ball at a time in the chocolate coating, use a fork to lift out, and return to the baking sheet. Continue with the remaining balls. Drizzle any remaining chocolate on top.

**6** Place in the fridge for at least 30 minutes, or until ready to serve. Store leftovers in the fridge for up to 2 weeks or in the freezer for up to 3 months.

**GLUTEN-FREE // VEGAN**

# MINUTE MUG CAKES

## FOR A LICKITY-SPLIT DESSERT

**BASE**

1 teaspoon virgin coconut oil

¼ cup almond meal

1 egg

2 tablespoons honey

¼ teaspoon baking powder

**MOCHA MADNESS**

1 teaspoon unsweetened cocoa powder

1 teaspoon ground coffee

1 tablespoon chocolate chips

**COCONUT-VANILLA**

2 tablespoons shredded coconut

½ teaspoon vanilla

**LEMON CHIA SEED**

2 teaspoons chia seeds

2 teaspoons lemon juice

We heard a rumor that single-serving cakes could be baked in the microwave in a minute. We had to try it ourselves. We wanted a gluten-free mini cake that was light and fluffy, yet sweetly satisfying. After mastering the first flavor, we just kept going until we ended up with three rock-star flavors. This recipe is so seriously easy you could make it in a dorm room. It also makes for a fun cooking project for kids.

Dress up your mug. We love to top this cake with a dollop of whole milk yogurt and chopped strawberries. It's a great energizing breakfast or dessert in a sweet pinch! **SERVES 1**

**1** Put the coconut oil in a microwave-safe mug and microwave just until melted, about 20 seconds. Add the almond meal, egg, honey, and baking powder, and stir to combine.

**2** Stir in the ingredients for your favorite flavor: Mocha Madness, Coconut-Vanilla, or Lemon Chia Seed.

**3** Microwave on high for 90 seconds. Let cool for 5 minutes. Devour with a spoon right out of the mug.

**GLUTEN-FREE // VEGETARIAN // DAIRY-FREE**

*"Use your head for the first half of the race and your heart for the second half."*

**—COACH**

# STRAWBERRY-RHUBARB CHIA PARFAIT
*FOR SWEET STAMINA*

### CHIA SEED PUDDING

1 cup plain whole milk yogurt

1 cup unsweetened almond milk

½ cup chia seeds

¼ cup honey

2 teaspoons vanilla

⅛ teaspoon fine sea salt

### STRAWBERRY-RHUBARB COMPOTE

3 cups quartered strawberries, stems removed (about 1 pound)*

2 cups (about 3 stalks) chopped rhubarb, ends discarded*

2 to 3 tablespoons honey, depending on sweetness of berries

2 tablespoons water

*When rhubarb and strawberries are not in season, sub in Sautéed Apples (page 77).*

Chia seeds should always be soaked in a liquid prior to consuming, since they can absorb 10 times their weight in water. We recommend making the pudding the night before serving.

Warning: This mighty dessert (or breakfast!) will make you want to run longer than your coach allows. Chia seeds may be tiny but they pack an incredible punch of micronutrients, omega-3 fatty acids, protein, and fiber. That's why they were the food of choice for Aztec and Mayan warriors. In fact, chia means "strength" in the Mayan language.

We love to serve this pretty parfait in half-pint glass jars. Go all out and top each parfait with Honey Cardamom Granola (page 64). **SERVES 5**

1  To make the pudding: In a medium bowl, combine the yogurt, milk, chia seeds, honey, vanilla, and salt.

2  Cover and refrigerate overnight (or for at least 2 hours).

3  To make the compote: In a medium saucepan, combine the strawberries, rhubarb, honey, and water. Simmer uncovered, stirring occasionally, until the rhubarb breaks down and the sauce thickens, about 15 minutes. Cool completely (will thicken) before assembling.

4  To assemble the parfait: Layer the chia pudding, then the strawberry-rhubarb compote in 4 or 5 half-pint glass jars. Repeat these layers a second time. If desired, top with granola or chopped nuts.

**GLUTEN-FREE // VEGETARIAN // DAIRY-FREE:** Use coconut milk yogurt.

# WARRIOR POPS
## FOR REFRESHING STAMINA

While pregnant in the heat of August, Elyse churned out a new Popsicle concoction on a weekly basis to share with her 3-year-old. Popsicles are a great vehicle for sneaking in some awesome nutrition. The addition of chia seeds adds stamina, omega-3s, protein, and fiber and gives the pops a dreamy consistency.

These two flavors quickly became beloved among the neighborhood kids. Try the Watermelon Berry flavor when you're craving something light and refreshing and the Coconut Milk Fudgesicles when you're hankering for creamy ice cream. **MAKES 6 POPSICLES**

---

2 heaping cups chopped watermelon (seedless)

1 cup frozen blueberries or raspberries

3 tablespoons honey (or maple syrup)

2 tablespoons chia seeds

Juice of 1 lime

### WATERMELON BERRY POPSICLES

In a blender, process the watermelon, berries, honey (or maple syrup), chia seeds, and lime juice until completely smooth. Divide among 6 Popsicle molds, add the sticks, and freeze overnight.

1 large or 2 small frozen bananas

1 cup canned full-fat coconut milk

½ cup coconut water

¼ cup unsweetened cocoa powder

3 tablespoons maple syrup

2 tablespoons chia seeds

### COCONUT MILK FUDGESICLES

In a blender, process the bananas, coconut milk, coconut water, cocoa powder, maple syrup, and chia seeds until smooth. Divide among 6 Popsicle molds, add the sticks, and freeze overnight.

**GLUTEN-FREE // VEGAN:** Use maple syrup instead of honey.

# 10 | RACE READY

*"In an ordinary training day, I remind myself
that I am preparing for the extraordinary."*

**–SHALANE**

# CHAI CASHEW BUTTER

*FOR LASTING ENERGY*

3 cups roasted cashews

3 tablespoons coconut sugar (or white sugar)

2 tablespoons virgin coconut oil

1½ teaspoons ground cinnamon

1 teaspoon ground ginger

1 teaspoon vanilla

¼ teaspoon fine sea salt (leave out if your nuts are salted)

Roast your own nuts to enhance their flavor and digestibility. See page 201 for directions. Just make sure the nuts have fully cooled before you blend into nut butter.

Nut butter is an easy-to-pack, digestible fuel source for before, during, or after long runs. We designed this nut butter to be delicious by the spoonful right out of the jar. You also can't go wrong slathering it on toast, bananas, or apple slices for a high-stamina snack. We also love to stir it into oatmeal for a sustaining breakfast. **MAKES 1¾ CUPS**

**1** In a food processor or high-speed blender, combine the cashews, sugar, coconut oil, cinnamon, ginger, vanilla, and salt.

**2** Process on high speed for several minutes until smooth, stopping as needed to scrape down the sides and underneath the blade.

**3** This nut butter is easier to spread when stored at room temperature. It will stay fresh in a glass jar in the pantry for up to 1 month. For a longer shelf life, store in the fridge for up to 3 months.

**GLUTEN-FREE // VEGAN**

"When I pin on my bib, I never put the pins through the designated holes. I always poke the pins through the bib itself so that it lies closer to my chest and is more aerodynamic. My dad taught me this little race ritual when I was a kid."

—SHALANE

# CHOCOLATE COCONUT CASHEW ENERGY BARS

*FOR SUSTAINED ENERGY*

2 cups pitted dates (Deglet Noor variety)*

1½ cups unsweetened shredded coconut

1 cup raw, unsalted cashews

⅓ cup unsweetened cocoa powder

2 tablespoons virgin coconut oil

¼ teaspoon fine sea salt

*If your dates are dry or old, rehydrate them by soaking briefly in warm water and patting dry.*

Elyse loves developing energizing new recipes for Picky Bars, a real-food bar company started by elite athletes Jesse Thomas, Lauren Fleshman, and Steph Bruce. Lucky for you, this fast crew agreed to give you a sneak peek of one of Elyse's tasty concoctions.

These little bars pack a mean punch, thanks to the power combo of dates for quick fuel and cashews and coconut oil for sustained energy. The cocoa powder provides antioxidants, minerals, and a little caffeine boost. And doubly awesome, this performance snack is free of refined sweeteners and processed protein powders, which can wreak havoc on your digestive system. **MAKES 16 BARS**

**1** In a food processor, combine the dates, coconut, cashews, cocoa, coconut oil, and salt. Pulse a few times to chop the ingredients and then process on high speed for 1 to 2 minutes, stopping once or twice to scrape down the sides of the bowl and underneath the blade. Process until the ingredients clump together.

**2** Line an 8 x 8-inch baking dish with parchment paper. Add the mixture and use your hands to spread out. Use a metal spatula to firmly press into an even layer filling the bottom of the dish. Chill for 30 minutes in the fridge and then slice into 16 bars (a pizza cutter works great).

**GLUTEN-FREE // VEGAN**

# ENERGY SQUEEZE

## FOR REAL FOOD MARATHON FUEL

½ cup mashed sweet
potato (yams; see cooking
instructions, page 141)

⅓ cup dates, finely
chopped

2 tablespoons peanut
butter (100% peanuts)

1 teaspoon chia seeds

⅛ teaspoon high-quality
sea salt

---

**Nutrition Facts**
As explained in
Chapter 1, we don't
provide nutrition facts on
recipes for several reasons,
but since runners need
consistency for race day
fuel, we've provided the
estimated stats for this
recipe. The recipe above
makes 3 servings, so scale
it up or down to suit your
energy needs.

**PER SERVING**
**Macronutrients:**
180 calories,
28 g carbohydrate
(14 g natural sugar),
6 g fat, 4 g protein

**Electrolytes:** 480 mg
potassium, 150 mg
sodium, 26 mg calcium,
33 mg magnesium

While on book tour, the number-one request we received was
recipes for whole-foods endurance fuel. Marathoners, triathletes,
and ultra runners are tired of the overly sweet gels and chews.
We created this option for those looking for an easy-to-digest
fuel that provides both quick and long-lasting energy.

Don't try anything new on race day. Test out this recipe multiple times on long training rides or runs and adjust it to fit your
needs. This fuel should be consumed with at least 8 ounces of
water or your favorite diluted hydration drink. Sea salt replaces
necessary electrolytes, and chia seeds help the body retain
fluids, but both can make you thirsty if you're not hydrating
while on the run. **MAKES 3 SERVINGS**

---

**1** In a small bowl, combine the sweet potato, dates, peanut
butter, 2 tablespoons water, chia seeds, and salt. Stir until well
mashed.

**2** Divide among 3 snack-size resealable bags. If consuming while
in motion, simply use your teeth to tear open a corner of the bag
and squeeze into your mouth. Alternatively, you can buy reusable
baby-food pouches, which are easy to fill and easy to eat from
while in motion.

**3** Store leftovers in the fridge for up to 5 days.

### CHOCOLATE TWIST

Add 2 tablespoons of unsweetened cocoa powder and 1 additional tablespoon of water to the above.

**GLUTEN-FREE // VEGAN**

*Shalane, Elyse, and friend Liz Holt, running a 12-mile loop on
Green Lakes trail on South Sister mountain in Oregon.*

"*Your body is not your masterpiece—your life is.*"

**–GLENNON DOYLE MELTON**

# MOLASSES GRANOLA BARS

### FOR TOPPING OFF YOUR ENERGY STORES

1½ cups old-fashioned rolled oats

½ cup unsweetened coconut flakes

⅓ cup unsweetened dried cherries, chopped

⅓ cup pumpkin seeds

¼ cup sesame seeds

1 teaspoon ground cinnamon

¼ teaspoon fine sea salt

½ cup tahini (or peanut butter)

3 tablespoons virgin coconut oil, melted

⅓ cup blackstrap molasses

1 teaspoon vanilla

Wrap them individually so you have a grab-n-go snack at the ready.

Can't sleep? You could be low in magnesium. These mineral-rich granola bars are a favorite of Shalane's with a cup of herbal tea. See more sleep tips on page 150.

These chewy and decadent allergy-friendly granola bars will convince you to stop buying sugary granola bars. You can feel good about devouring this satisfying snack, which is high in healthy fats and minerals. Pumpkin and sesame seeds are rich in magnesium, which is essential for muscle function, bone health, sleep, and so much more (basically every cell in the body needs magnesium to function properly). The molasses adds a dose of iron that would make Popeye proud.

Shalane likes to snack on these bars to top off her glycogen stores in the week leading up to a race. They are high in fiber so are not intended for race day fuel. (Don't say we didn't warn you!)

**MAKES 16 SQUARES**

**1** Preheat the oven to 350°F. Line an 8 x 8-inch baking dish with parchment paper.

**2** In a large bowl, mix together the oats, coconut, cherries, pumpkin seeds, sesame seeds, cinnamon, and salt.

**3** Add the tahini (or peanut butter), melted coconut oil, molasses, and vanilla and stir (use your muscles) to combine. Spoon into the baking dish and use a metal spatula to press down firmly into a compact, even layer.

**4** Bake in the center of the oven for 25 to 30 minutes, or until the top is firm and slightly darker. Remove from the oven and let cool completely. Once cool, use the parchment paper to lift out and transfer to a cutting board. Use a sharp knife to cut into 16 bars.

**GLUTEN-FREE:** Use certified gluten-free oats. // **VEGAN**

# LEMON GINGERADE

**FOR DIGESTION-ENHANCING HYDRATION**

4 cups filtered water

2-inch piece fresh ginger, peeled and grated

¼ cup fresh lemon juice

2 tablespoons honey

⅛ teaspoon fine sea salt (optional)

Digestive ailments are a commonality among runners (as evidenced by the long porta-john lines at races!). When you're putting in the miles, oxygen flows away from your digestive system to your hardworking muscles, which can compromise digestion.

Ginger and lemon juice reawaken your digestive tract. Ginger is a natural carminative (relieves flatulence) and intestinal spasmolytic (relaxes and soothes). Before you're tempted to inhale a meal after a long run, sip on this refreshing drink (and remember—eat slowly). Rock solid digestion enables your body to maximize nutrient absorption, which is essential to overall health and happiness.

While training at high altitude in Mammoth for the NYC Marathon, Shalane made up a batch of this brew every week to sip the day before her long training runs. For an additional electrolyte boost, she likes to add coconut water. **MAKES 4 CUPS**

---

**1** Bring the water to a boil in a pot over high heat. Place the grated ginger in a tea ball or directly in the pot. Turn the heat to low, cover, and simmer for 15 minutes.

**2** Remove the tea ball or pour through a strainer into an iced-tea pitcher or widemouthed quart glass jar. Stir in the lemon juice, honey, and salt (if using). Chill in the fridge and serve over ice.

**GLUTEN-FREE // VEGETARIAN // VEGAN:** Use maple syrup instead of honey.

"I always get a haircut and have my nails painted before a big race. It's a relaxing ritual and helps me feel sleek, feminine, and confident."

**–SHALANE**

# SHALANE'S NATURAL SPORTS DRINK

**FOR SERIOUS HYDRATION**

2 cups filtered water

2 cups coconut water

½ cup tart cherry juice (optional)*

2 tablespoons fresh-squeezed lemon juice

1 tablespoon blackstrap molasses

¼ teaspoon high-quality sea salt

*Juices are high in sugar, which is why we always dilute them with water and use them in small quantities, mainly just for flavoring. If you can't find tart cherry juice, sub in any other favorite juice.*

Never try anything new on race day. Everyone's fuel and hydration needs vary greatly, so it's important to test out your race day nutrition during training to find what works best for you.

You don't need to down a neon-blue beverage to make it to the finish line faster. If you're in search of a natural sports drink, experiment with our race-ready concoction below. We hand-selected each ingredient to maximize electrolyte replenishment (potassium, sodium, calcium, magnesium) and provide simple carbs for quick energy. **MAKES 28 OUNCES**

>> **Coconut water:** high in potassium and magnesium, quick glucose boost

>> **Tart cherry juice:** high in potassium with anti-inflammatory and antioxidant properties

>> **Blackstrap molasses:** high in iron, calcium, and magnesium

>> **Sea salt:** replenishes sodium lost in sweat and other essential trace minerals

**1** In an iced-tea pitcher or half-gallon glass jar, combine the water, coconut water, cherry juice (if using), lemon juice, molasses, and salt. Seal the jar with a lid and shake vigorously to combine. Store in the fridge for up to 3 days.

**2** For long runs, drink 16 ounces 1 hour prior to running.

**GLUTEN-FREE // VEGAN**

# WARRIOR DRINK
## FOR POST-WORKOUT HYDRATION

1 cup coconut water

1 cup tart cherry juice*

1 cup filtered water

Juice of 1 lime

2 tablespoons chia seeds

⅛ teaspoon high-quality sea salt

*Since juice is high in sugar, we dilute this drink with water. Feel free to add more water to suit your sweetness preference. If you can't find tart cherry juice, sub in any other favorite juice.*

After a serious sweat session, you may need more than just water to rehydrate. We created this refreshing drink to help replenish electrolytes without all the additives found in most sports beverages. Coconut water is high in potassium, tart cherry juice is high in antioxidants, and sea salt is high in electrolytes and trace minerals.

The addition of chia seeds adds a healthy dose of omega-3 fatty acids, protein, fiber, and minerals. In ancient times, chia seeds were the survival food of Aztec warriors. Chia seeds expand in liquids, helping your body retain fluids. **MAKES 24 OUNCES**

**1** In a quart-size glass jar, combine the coconut water, cherry juice, water, lime juice, chia seeds, and salt. Seal tightly with the lid and shake to combine.

**2** Chill for 15 minutes or longer in the fridge to allow the chia seeds to gel. Shake again just before drinking.

**GLUTEN-FREE // VEGAN**

# APPLE GINGER GELATIN
## FOR PROTEIN GEL SHOTS

1½ cups unfiltered apple juice

2 tablespoons beef gelatin powder*

½ cup boiling water

½-inch piece ginger, peeled and finely grated (about 1 teaspoon)

*Look for a high-quality, grass-fed brand of pure beef collagen. We like Great Lakes Unflavored Gelatin (red canister) or Vital Proteins Beef Gelatin.

This gelatin is not very sweet. If you prefer a sweeter version, stir in a tablespoon of honey with the ginger.

Protein powders are highly processed, hard on our digestive systems, and not easily absorbed. Plus, they're often full of a lot of additives that our bodies don't love. Shalane does not use any protein supplements, not even during her peak training, and instead prefers to get all her protein from real food sources.

But if you must have a protein supplement, the one we feel provides the most bioavailable, complete protein is beef gelatin powder (collagen). Studies show collagen promotes joint health, maintains healthy bones, and can help reduce recovery time after a long run. It's also gut-soothing, especially with the addition of ginger. Since it gels in liquid, we like to make it into gelatin squares for a tasty treat that reminds us of the Jell-O of yester-year, but without the artificial flavoring and coloring. **SERVES 2**

**1**  In a medium bowl, use a fork to whisk together ½ cup of the juice with the gelatin until fully dissolved. Let sit for 1 minute. Stir in the boiling water. Add the remaining 1 cup of juice and ginger and whisk again.

**2**  Pour into an 8 x 8-inch baking dish. Place in the fridge for at least 1 hour or overnight. Cut into cubes and use a spatula to transfer to bowls.

**GLUTEN-FREE**

# ANTI-INFLAMMATORY CHOCOLATE "MILK"

## FOR A BETTER RECOVERY DRINK

2 cups coconut water

2 tablespoons almond butter or peanut butter

4 dates, pitted, or 1 tablespoon blackstrap molasses

1 tablespoon unsweetened cocoa powder

1-inch piece fresh ginger, peeled

1-inch piece fresh turmeric, peeled (optional)

1 cup ice

Endurance athletes adore chocolate milk as a post-workout recovery drink. The problem with store-bought chocolate milk is that it's loaded with sugar and made with ultrapasteurized and homogenized milk, which is difficult to digest.

We created this dairy-free alternative that will quickly replenish your electrolytes and glycogen stores, thanks to the coconut water and dates or molasses. The anti-inflammatory cocoa powder, ginger, and turmeric take it to the next level. **SERVES 2**

**1** In a blender, combine the coconut water, nut butter, dates or molasses, cocoa powder, ginger, turmeric (if using), and ice. Blend on high speed for several minutes until smooth.

**2** Store in a glass jar in the fridge for up to 3 days.

**3** If you prefer a thicker, smoothie-type consistency, add in 1 frozen banana.

**GLUTEN-FREE // VEGAN**

"*Remember. A setback is just a setup for a comeback.*"

**–SHALANE,**
*AFTER WINNING THE TCS NEW YORK CITY MARATHON 9 MONTHS AFTER A MAJOR INJURY*

# SHALANE'S TOP 10 RACE TIPS

**1** >> **TRAIN THE BRAIN** In the midst of hard workouts I like to practice pushing through the discomfort and pain that I will inevitably feel on race day. I use mantras to help myself focus and live in the moment. For example, I may chant to myself "You got this!" Or think about inspirational quotes like, "You don't train to feel your best, you train to be at your best when you feel your worst."

**2** >> **CROSS-TRAIN** To prevent injury or burnout, I like to get in extra cardiovascular work by lifting weights, swimming or aqua jogging, and stationary cycling. I sometimes replace my afternoon (second) run with one of these if I am feeling flat.

**3** >> **FUEL RIGHT** Proper hydration and fuel every day is vital to racing success. Not just eating right in the week leading up to race day. During peak training, cooking wholesome meals helps me recover, makes me happy, and enhances my training. My race-day meal consists of a large bowl of oatmeal with almond milk, honey, walnuts or almonds, bananas, and raspberries or blueberries. I also have to have my coffee and my sports drink (see page 233 for our Shalane's Natural Sports Drink recipe).

**4** >> **NOTHING NEW ON RACE DAY** Preparation is key in preventing race-day surprises. I practice every detail including what underwear I will race in! I practice my prerace meals, shoes, uniform, sports drink, etc. Never try anything new on race day!!

**5** >> **THE LONG RUN IS ESSENTIAL** The staple workout in my marathon training is the long run. I run anywhere from 20 to 28 miles every 7 to 10 days during my peak season. This provides huge fitness gains as well as confidence that I can go the distance. For those racing shorter distances like a 5K, their long run might be 8 to 10 miles.

**6** >> **BE FLEXIBLE** Set goals and share them! I set three goals for every race: Goals A, B, and C (in case something goes wrong). On any given day your best thought-out plan can unravel, so it's important to not panic midrace. Goal A is the perfect day, then B is my next best scenario, and so on. This keeps me focused when things get tough as they did at the 2016 Olympic Marathon Trials. I was able to dig deep and stick to Goal C instead of giving up. This focus enabled me to make my fourth Olympic team.

**7** >> **SIMULATE THE COURSE** Some race courses have lots of turns and hills, while others are flat and fast. I like to do my homework and try to simulate my own version where I live and train so that my body and mind are prepared.

**8** >> **TAPER** It's time to peak! This means gradually dialing back your training before the race (for a marathon, I recommend a 3-week taper period). Some people suffer from "taper tantrums" and feel they are becoming unfit. I like to take this time to get extra sleep and imagine all the energy my body is storing up for race day! If I am restless and need distractions, I meet up with friends for coffee.

**9** >> **GET YOUR ZZZZS** I can tell when I'm not getting enough sleep because I start to get grumpy, I can't focus, and my legs feel stale. I shoot for 9 hours every night and sneak in a nap during the day between my training sessions. Sleep allows the body to recover fully and repair itself, which is crucial during intense training. See sleep tips on page 150.

**10** >> **RACE SHORT TO BOOST FITNESS** Racing a 5K, 10K, or half marathon is a great way to keep me motivated while training for a marathon. It's also a good fitness test and lets me know where I am in my training.

# YOUR REAL FOOD STORIES
## (LETTERS FROM YOU)

Hello Shalane and Elyse,
I'm a Division I Cross-Country and Track athlete. I received your cookbook as a Christmas gift from my father, and it has changed my relationship with food. When I started running at the collegiate level, I started obsessing over my caloric intake, losing lots of weight in the process, and becoming a firm believer that thin equals fast. While my times sure did drop in the beginning, it was not a sustainable approach. I developed anemia and athletic amenorrhea and later on, two stress fractures. More important, I was unhappy, tired of monitoring every food choice, exhausted from all the grueling workouts, which were run on virtually no fuel, and frustrated that my performances had taken a nosedive. Indulging in real foods helped me regain my health and eventually train and perform better. I no longer looked at food as the enemy; rather, it became indulgent nourishment, something I looked forward to, something my body deserved after all the hard work I'd put it through. Thanks for the great recipes and all the joy and happiness that your book has brought back into my life.

Sincerely,
Annais, 21 years old
Tenafly, New Jersey

*Shalane and Elyse with a group of young fans at a book tour event hosted by Fleet Feet in Chapel Hill, North Carolina.*

Elyse,

My sister-in-law bought your cookbook for my daughter, Hannah. It has been the best gift! Hannah is a high school runner. In 8th to 10th grades, she was starting off well with cross-country but was having these weird spells of no energy. As her mom, I just felt like her energy should be more consistent. In addition to dealing with some hypoglycemic episodes, I was trying to encourage Hannah to eat better. She took it too far and lost too much weight as she was increasing her training (avoiding carbs). Her high school actually called me with concerns about anorexia. Hannah (not a reader) read your cookbook cover to cover the day it arrived and absorbed everything you said about the needs of a female runner. Our whole family has enjoyed the recipes and the lessons learned along the way about nutrition and quality ingredients.

Hannah had her best cross-country season and is excited about the opportunities to run in college. She is now very curious about nutrition and cooking. She even talks about going to culinary school! As a teenager, she impresses me with her willingness to plan ahead and cook for herself and our whole family. She is way ahead of where I was at that age.

This is a scary time as a parent when your children go to the Internet for information. They don't know yet that everything on the Internet is not good information, as evidenced by what happened to my daughter.

Thank you for putting good information out there through writing *Run Fast. Eat Slow*.!!

Kimberly, 42 years old
Charlotte, North Carolina

*Shalane and Elyse speaking at a book tour event hosted by Footzone in Bend, Oregon.*

Life.Changing.Folks!

I'm surely not the fastest out there, but as my adventures with the book happened to coincide with a new training plan for a half-marathon in April, I can vouch for improved overall health and a shiny new 6:30 PR, as well as a much easier recovery than in prior races of that distance.

My little people, aged 7 and 8 currently, use this cookbook to help with the weekly meal planning. The photography is key to them, as they'll pick something just based on the beautiful picture and one ingredient that they know they love!

This fabulous cookbook has improved our house! Mom, age 39, still knocking out PRs and having a fabulous course in training, no doubt in part due to correct nutrition; Dad, age 37, expanding his tastes even further; kidlets, ages 7 and 8, INVOLVED in nutrition and LOVING family meal planning.

Thank you sincerely,
Courtney, 39 years old
Michigan

*Shalane and Elyse leading a Nike Run Club run in Central Park during their book tour.*

Hey Elyse,

I purchased your cookbook back in February and my husband and I decided to cook our way through it. We absolutely love the meals and had a blast cooking with real foods and full fats! Much to our surprise, we found out last week that we are 8 weeks pregnant! I 100 percent believe this was possible by changing our diet! We had just been told by fertility doctors that our only option was artificial insemination or IVF. So thanks for all your help thus far!

Elisabeth, 25 years old
Coaldale, Alberta

Hi Shalane and Elyse,

In the summer before my 9th grade year, I began to eat very little, even while logging intense runs. This was mostly as a result of hearing people (including relatives who had previously been runners) and publications tell me that, to be a good runner, I must be extremely skinny, and the fact that many of the other girls on our varsity squad naturally have very thin bodies (whereas my body type is more muscular than it is thin). Thankfully, a coach noticed that I was rapidly losing weight before things could get out of hand. Despite that, the past several years have been rocky, as I hear so many things about how being stick-thin is absolutely necessary for the best runners, and I would often restrict myself from foods that I loved so that I could prevent myself from gaining weight.

This year, around the beginning of track season, I saw the *Run Fast. Eat Slow.* feature in the *Runner's World* magazine. Drawn by the delicious-looking recipes and Shalane's success running off them, I ordered the book and was immediately enticed by the incredible recipes but, most of all, by the introduction. I was surprised to find that, even at the professional level, Shalane herself eats sweets and high-fat foods (which I had previously dismissed as "unhealthy") to sustain her running.

*Run Fast. Eat Slow.* has made a world of difference in how I perceive food and eating and has let me discover that healthy should never mean restrictive. Thank you so much for this opportunity and, most of all, for creating a cookbook that teaches girls like me that being skinny and being healthy are in no way correlated. This cookbook has been a major part in my recovery from the awful, negative thoughts that I experienced even a year and a half after my disordered eating had stopped. I hope that you keep on pushing to make delicious recipes that will keep generations of runners full of good food and fast splits!

Sincerely,
Sarah, 16 years old
Albuquerque, New Mexico

---

Good evening,
I don't even know where to begin with how Shalane and Elyse have changed my life. I'll start by introducing you to my past . . . about 4 years ago, I was suffering with severe pain in my shins. After endless doctor visits, physical therapy sessions, X-rays, and painful runs, I was diagnosed with severe stress fractures along my right tibia. I was at the peak of my running career and stopping didn't seem possible for me—especially because I was struggling with an eating disorder at the time.

After being forced into treatment, I was thankfully able to recover, but I couldn't have done it without the endless support from my family and friends.

For 4 years, I was terrified to run again. I thought that I was weak and wasn't made for running. I couldn't understand how some people could run 10 miles or more a day and not get injured, while I got injured from running 5 a day.

After reading Shalane and Elyse's stories in *Run Fast. Eat Slow.* and then watching Shalane push through her own injury, I knew I had to try again. Their inspiring stories motivated me and made me want to do what I've always loved to do: run.

Not only were their stories motivating, but the recipes were to die for—they gave me the nutrition I needed AND they were delicious!

In all honesty, I wouldn't be where I am today without Shalane and Elyse. Just last week, I ran my first race in 4 years. It was also my first 10K—something I never thought I'd be able to do. They taught me that nobody's perfect—even professionals. We all get hurt, we all have our struggles, but it's the ones who persevere that survive.

Thank you so much for taking the time to read my story. I hope I'm able to share this with other runners and athletes who are facing the same battles that I was able to overcome.

Bryanna, 20 years old
Westbrook, Maine

---

Dear Elyse,
I just wanted to email back and say that after really focusing on adding more healthy fats to my diet the past 5 months (so many avocados!), I have naturally had two periods this fall. This occurred after completing my highest mileage marathon training season. After many years of seeing doctors and never once hearing about diet changes, I am so thankful to you and Shalane for shedding light on this issue. I cannot wait for more *Run Fast. Eat Slow.* recipes and miles!

Congratulations on the newest addition to your family and Happy Thanksgiving!

Best,
Grace, 24 years old
South Bend, Indiana

# *ACKNOWLEDGMENTS*

**TOGETHER** we would like to express supreme gratitude to the dream team behind *Run Fast. Cook Fast. Eat Slow.*, including:

Everyone at Rodale Books who believed in our book from day one and worked tirelessly to launch our second book prior to Rodale becoming an imprint of Penguin Random House. We are especially grateful to Maria Rodale for all that she's done for the health and wellness book industry over the past thirty years.

Our energetic team at Penguin Random House and Harmony Books, who wholeheartedly invited us into the family and believed in this important movement. Endless thank-yous to Diana Baroni, Kathryn Santora, Tammy Blake, Christina Foxley, Estefania Ospina, Michele Eniclerico, Terry Deal, Philip Leung, and Mia Johnson.

Our dedicated editor, Dervla Kelly, and diligent marketing liaison, Brianne Sperber, who both willingly packed their offices to join us at our new home at Penguin Random House. Thank you for your love and support over the years.

Our compassionate agent, Danielle Svetcov, who continues to be our guiding light, coach, and friend on this incredible journey. We have the best agent on the best coast.

Our cookbook assistant, Natalie Bickford, who is a whiz in the kitchen, an expert nutritionist, and a diligent worker bee. Thank you for moving to Bend, Oregon, to reunite with us for this second book.

Brilliant cookbook designer, Rae Ann Spitzenberger, who brought to life our vision and took it to a whole new level of awesomeness.

Our talented photographer, Alan Weiner, who has patiently and energetically followed us around and put up with our silliness on set through two books.

The incredible food stylist, Ashley Marti, and dedicated tech lead, A. J. Meeker. Thank you for joining our team again. You are the reason every food photo in this book looks beyond delicious.

Brasada Ranch, for hosting us on their gorgeous property for our Bend photoshoot.

*Runner's World* friends, including Heather Mayer Irvine, Bart Yasso, and David Willey.

Aly Mostel, star cookbook publicist, who

*Shalane and Elyse with cookbook assistant Natalie Bickford, eating lunch at The Lot food carts in Bend, Oregon.*

worked her magic to organize all of our media and events for the first book and continues to be our biggest cheerleader.

Our team of recipe testers, who helped us take each recipe to the next level, including Matt Llano, Gwen Jorgensen, Anne Bennett Osteen, Christina Nee, Emma Marie Astrike-Davis, Travis and Lydia Gaylord, Marie Billen, Kelly Devlin, Ava Cummings, Gina Pardi, Julie Stackhouse, Ally Ringer, and Brittany Williams. And a special shout-out to our lead recipe tester, Michael Weisberg, who happily volunteered to eat every single recipe in this book.

This second cookbook would not have been possible without the incredible energy from our fans, who shared *Run Fast. Eat Slow.* with all their friends, posted delicious photos on Instagram, and continually asked us to write another book. We are grateful for this unwavering support from the running community.

### SHALANE THANKS . . .

My ride-or-die husband, Steve, for always dropping everything to support my dreams and goals. Your unwavering love and support gives me strength to go after audacious ideas.

Bowerman Babes, thank you for your insatiable hunger and for gobbling up our recipes in their early formation. It makes my heart smile when you send me pictures at training camp of your *Run Fast. Eat Slow.* creations. Fueling the ones I love to be world-class athletes and humans is the greatest feeling. You motivate me every single day. I love that all I have to do is look to my left and right for my inspiration.

My parents, for encouraging their kids to be fiercely independent and allowing us to just be us. Thank you for showing me how much you love me and how proud you are of Elyse and I.

My coaches, Jerry Schumacher and Pascal Dobert, for always believing in me, through broken bones to big-city marathon wins.

Makenna Schumacher, for joining me in the kitchen to recipe test and for being a devout Superhero Muffin baker!

The Running Community, for your faith, loving support, and encouragement.

Elyse, my shero. Your drive, passion, and determination are scary. Whatever you decide to pour your heart into, it turns to gold. It's been a privilege to watch you become the most loving and beautiful mother to Lily and Rylan. I know in my heart that you fueled me with our friendship and recipes toward that magical win in NYC. Thank you. The best is yet to come, my lovely.

## ELYSE THANKS . . .

My two adorable kiddos, Lily and Rylan, who are my biggest pride and joy: Watching you grow into strong, healthy, happy kids fueled by incredible food is what keeps me cooking every day. I will always cherish the many hours you both spent in your first year strapped to me in the kitchen while recipe testing for book one and book two. Thank you for making our kitchen the heart of our home.

My husband, Andy Hughes, who didn't flinch when I wanted to quit a successful marketing career and spend our savings on culinary school. I never would have taken this huge plunge into the unknown without your unwavering support. Thank you for encouraging me every step of the way. You're also the best-looking dishwasher in the world.

Grandma, Caren Arlas, who brings joy and laughter to our children. I could not have written this book while taking care of two little ones without your gracious help.

My sister, Jessa Lyders, whose journey and perseverance to bring two beautiful girls into this world is what ultimately inspired me to write these important cookbooks.

Bestie, Brittany Williams, who volunteered to edit my rough first draft while I was scrambling to finish the recipe testing before baby Ry was born.

And, most important, Shalane Flanagan, who inspired a nation when she won the NYC Marathon in 2017. Seeing you finally achieve your lifelong dream brought tears to my eyes. I'll never forget Lily, at three years old, exclaiming, "Mommy, happy and tears don't make sense together." Oh, but sometimes they do! I'm so grateful for our friendship over these last 18 years from our Green Street roomie days to sharing hotel rooms across the country during our book tour. When two ambitious women join forces and believe wholeheartedly in an important cause, mountains are moved. Thank you for believing in this book when it was just the tiniest of dreams. Smooches!

## A NOTE ON THE PHOTOS

The photos for this book were taken over a period of time. The outdoor photos were taken in Bend, Oregon, when Elyse was 7 months pregnant and prior to Shalane winning the NYC Marathon. The maternity photos were taken when Elyse was 38 weeks pregnant. The kitchen photos were taken at Shalane's house in Portland, Oregon, just after she won the NYC Marathon and Elyse was 2 months postpartum. The event photos were taken during the book tour for our first book.

# INDEX

Note: Page references in *italics* indicate photographs.

# ABOUT THE AUTHORS

**SHALANE FLANAGAN** is an Olympic silver medalist, four-time Olympian, 2017 TCS New York City Marathon champion, World Cross Country Bronze medalist, and multiple American record holder. She is the third fastest American marathoner in history, with a time of 2:21.14. Shalane is the fastest American woman to run the Boston Marathon, 2:22.02. Along with her coauthor, Elyse Kopecky, she is the *New York Times* bestselling author of *Run Fast. Eat Slow.: Nourishing Recipes for Athletes*.

Nike has sponsored Shalane since she graduated from the University of North Carolina at Chapel Hill in 2004. She has been running at an elite level for over 17 years and typically runs 100-plus miles a week. She attributes her ability to sustain this level of training to her nutrient-dense diet. Focusing on fueling for health and performance is an integral part of her training.

Shalane has been featured on the cover of *Runner's World*, *Women's Running*, *Running Times*, *Competitor Magazine*, and *Track and Field News*. She has appeared on the *Today* show, *Good Morning America*, *Live with Kelly and Ryan*, *60 Minutes*, *ESPN*, and *Oprah*. Her inspiring story has also been heralded in *Women's Health*, *Shape*, *USA Today*, the *Boston Globe*, and the *New York Times*. Shalane speaks passionately about the importance of healthy eating at running events across the country. Shalane lives and trains in Portland, Oregon. Follow her on Instagram @shalaneflanagan or at runfasteatslow.com.

*Shalane, all smiles, just minutes after winning the TCS New York City Marathon!*

**ELYSE KOPECKY** is a *New York Times* bestselling author, chef, nutrition coach, and inspirational speaker. Her friendship with Shalane began over 18 years ago on the cross-country team at the University of North Carolina. After graduation, both moved to Portland, Oregon, to work for Nike—Shalane as a professional runner, and Elyse as a digital marketing producer.

Elyse's career took her abroad, where she attended cooking classes throughout Europe, Africa, and Asia. Armed with amazing recipes from around the world, Elyse began cooking to fuel her athletic endeavors. She discovered that by incorporating more fats into her diet, she was stronger, healthier, and happier than ever before. She quit a successful marketing career of 10 years for the chance to help others eat right, and moved to New York City to study at the Natural Gourmet Institute for Health and Culinary Arts.

Elyse's idea for *Run Fast. Eat Slow.* began as a small dream over a home-cooked meal at Shalane's house. She never imagined it would become a *New York Times* bestseller, get translated into multiple languages, and be featured in *Runner's World, Women's Running, Outside Magazine*, and *Good Morning America*, to name a few.

Elyse lives in Bend, Oregon, with her husband, two sweet kids, and one rambunctious pup. She can be found at IndulgentNourishment.com and on Instagram @elysekopecky.